Dear
Janet,

God Bless!
As you read
story of Debbie.
was such a sweet P

Love Always
Lynn

MW01595152

Deborah Anne, God's Blessing

Dealing with the Loss of a Child

By

Lynn Stephens

authorHOUSE™

1663 LIBERTY DRIVE, SUITE 200
BLOOMINGTON, INDIANA 47403
(800) 839-8640
WWW.AUTHORHOUSE.COM

First published by AuthorHouse 05/18/05

ISBN: 1-4208-3188-7 (sc)

Printed in the United States of America
Bloomington, Indiana

This book is printed on acid-free paper.

TABLE OF CONTENTS

DEDICATION

I dedicate this book to the memory of our daughter
who was truly a blessing to her family.

DEBORAH ANNE STEPHENS
12/23/62 – 10/30/96

And to

Bradley Thomas
&
Katherine Anne
Her children who have had to go on without their
mother and their friend and do so
magnificently with the Lord's blessings!

To
Raymond Wayne Stephens,
her friend and her brother,
who is missing her as we all are.

To
her first husband, Tom,who is now raising
Bradley and Katherine in Illinois.

To
her husband, Charles, at the time
Deborah passed away.
May the Lord comfort them all.

FOREWORD

I am writing this book for several reasons and maybe for some I have not yet discovered. The loss of a child, whether young or old, is something that is almost indescribable and something which we are never prepared for. Yet, one of the reasons for writing this book is to help others with the loss of a child. The second reason is to write a testimony of God's love for his children and their seed. The third, but not the final, is to tell of the life of a very special young woman named Deborah Anne.

As you read through this book, you will see God's hand upon Deborah Anne's life and the lives of her family. You will see faith and the supernatural working of the Holy Spirit in the lives of this family.

In attempting to describe the life of my daughter, you will discover the inner most feelings of a mother throughout the life of that daughter.

It is my sincere desire that you would reach into your own feelings for your children, siblings and/or parents. We need to have a greater understanding, patience, and most importantly LOVE with those in our immediate families.

I would be remiss not to mention that Deborah Anne has a wonderful brother, Raymond Wayne Stephens, but that will be another story at a later time. But for now, Wayne and Lynn could not have asked for our son to turn out any different than he did. Ray, you are very special and have given me great inspiration for writing this story about your sister, Deborah Anne. Thanks must also go to Wayne, my wonderful husband, who is always my best critic.

THANK YOU GOD FOR BLESSING ME
From a Mother's Heart
By Lynn Stephens

THANK YOU GOD FOR BLESSING ME,
WITH THIS LITTLE GIRL THAT I CAN SEE.
I CHERISHED EACH MOMENT
WE HAD TOGETHER,
SHE CERTAINLY CHANGES
LIKE THE WEATHER.
SHE'S GROWN NOW INTO A
MOTHER AND WIFE,
WITH HER OWN LOVING FAMILY
SHARING HER LIFE.

THERE ARE A FEW THINGS I
WOULD HAVE DONE
IF I HAD BEEN WALKING WITH YOUR SON.
I WOULD HAVE TAUGHT HER
OF YOUR SPECIAL LOVE,
HOW MUCH GREATER THAN
MINE YOUR LOVE WAS.
I WOULD HAVE TOLD HER
ABOUT YOUR SON, JESUS,
WHO ONCE WE BELIEVED WOULD
TRULY RECEIVE US.
BUT NOW, DEAR LORD, I CAN
ONLY SUBMIT HER,
TO YOU IN PRAYER WHICH I
DAILY COMMIT HER.

SHE IS ALL GROWN NOW, MY LITTLE GIRL,
A FINE LOOKING WOMAN, A DEFINITE PEARL.
SHE IS KIND AND GENTLE LIKE
A WOMAN SHOULD BE,
SHE IS STRONG-WILLED AND
SMART WHAT A JOY TO SEE.
SHE IS NICE TO BE WITH AND
LOVINGLY FUNNY,
WE ARE VERY GOOD FRIENDS,
BUT NOT ALWAYS SUNNY.

A GOOD MOTHER AND WIFE,
I'M PROUD TO SAY,
SHE IS A COMFORT TO ME IN
HER OWN SPECIAL WAY.
I MISS AND AM LONELY
WHEN WE ARE APART,
AND MISS HER COMPANIONSHIP
FROM THE DEPTH OF MY HEART.
I RESPECT HER NEW FAMILY
WHO LOVES HER SO MUCH,
AND CHERISH THEIR HAPPINESS
I SEE AND THEIR TRUST.

I LOOK AT MY DAUGHTER WHO
IS CREATED BY YOU,
AND UNDERSTAND YOUR LOVE FOR ME TOO.
HOW YOU NEVER LEFT ME
AND NEVER GOT MAD,
EVEN THOUGH YOU KNEW
MY NATURE WAS BAD.

I HOPE WITH YOUR HELP, I'LL BE
THE MOTHER SHE NEEDS,
THAT MY LOVE WILL BE UNSELFISH
AND PATIENT IN DEEDS.
I AM THANKFUL TO YOU, LORD,
FOR ANSWERING MY PRAYER,
AS SHE BELONGED TO YOU, THROUGH YOUR
SON, WHEN HER FINAL JOURNEY SHE DARED.
THANK YOU, GOD, FOR MAKING ME SEE,
HOW TO LOVE THAT DAUGHTER
THAT YOU GAVE TO ME.

CHAPTER ONE
OUR LITTLE GIRL

It is 1:30 PM Wednesday, October 30, 1996. I am standing by Deborah's bed in ICU at Northwest Hospital in Tucson, Arizona. Wayne and I had just been advised nothing more could be done for Debbie and they recommended we take her off the respirator. As tears accumulated in our eyes, we prayed over her and gave her to the Lord. He would either heal her or take her home to be with Him, which of course would be the ultimate healing. We made the decision not to take her off the respirator until we could get the family to return to the hospital, especially her children Bradley and Katherine. Wayne went to call the family back to the hospital by 5 PM. I laid my head in my daughter's lap, thanking the Lord for the gift of having her in our lives for 33 years. What a blessing she was. I drifted back to 1962 when her life began—

I met and married my husband, her dad, on February 3, 1962, at 2 PM at the Fort Leonard Wood Chapel in

Missouri. Lt. Wayne R. Stephens was a striking young officer in the United States Army. He was an infantry officer, six feet tall, with sea-blue color eyes, and pale, blonde hair in a crew cut. My father, Col. Raymond W. Beggs, was Chief of Staff of the army post at the time we got married; he and my mother, Marie, lived in quarters on post. Madeleine Jane Beggs was my maiden name, but everyone called me Lynn. As we united as one that beautiful, warm, winter day, we had all the hopes and dreams of every couple that is joined in matrimony. We had a military wedding with all the trimmings and a beautiful reception at the Officers Club on Post. We honeymooned in St. Louis, Missouri, as we had little money in those days. A second lieutenant, living on post, brought in $375.00 a month, plus housing and medical benefits. We were in love and it was sufficient.

A month after we were married and situated in our quarters on post, Wayne got notified that he was would be going to Jungle Warfare School in Panama. We had two weeks before he left, and as a young bride, I was frightened for his safety because I knew this was a tough school. We decided to try for a child in the two weeks before he left. It may have been foolish thinking on our part, but being in love, all I could think of was to have his child in case he didn't come home. He was an only child, and I wanted his legacy to be carried on.

I must insert here, that our faith was in God; we knew of Jesus as the Savior of the world but had not accepted him personally, nor did we have an intimate relationship with the Trinity. When I was eleven years old, my parents took me to see Billy Graham at Madison Square Garden. At the invitation, I wanted to go forward, but my parents wouldn't go forward as they didn't find it necessary. I could not go by myself as we were sitting high up in the arena. They were Presbyterians and thought that was enough. So, I feel now, looking back, that I turned my heart toward the Lord that day but did not know how to progress in my Christian walk. Consequently, I had a searching desire the rest of my life and knew I was empty of something

3

until I met Jesus in 1982. I had been brought up in church and was taught to be good was enough. Wayne's family members were church-hoppers when they went. Lutheran and Methodist was mainly his background, but his family would leave churches when something did not go their way. Confused about God would be a good definition of where we were in our spiritual life.

Wayne did return from Panama, and I was with child. Deborah Anne was born at eleven in the morning on December 23, 1962. She was beautiful, having the same sea-blue eyes and pale, blonde hair that her father had. Her skin was all pink, rosy, and smooth not looking at all like a newborn. Wayne was so proud of his little, baby girl and couldn't take his eyes off her. We brought her home the day after Christmas, and my parents came over and we celebrated the season a day late. It was a special Christmas because a child was in the house, and no matter how old they are, it still makes the event special. It was also our first Christmas as Lt. and Mrs. Wayne R. Stephens. Joy! Joy! There was plenty of joy.

1963 held a big trip in Deborah's young life. Wayne received orders for Fort Richardson in Anchorage, Alaska. For the months of January and February, we studied all we could about Alaska. Because we had a dog, a German Shepherd named Cocoa, people who had already made the trip advised us to get to McCord Air Force Base in Washington at least a week before our scheduled flight. It sometimes took a week to make arrangements for your pet to be flown to Alaska on a commercial flight. During this time, we also celebrated our first wedding anniversary on the 3rd of February. In March (Debbie was now two and a half months old), we packed up our household things and shipped them ahead. As we made the trip to McCord Air Force Base after visiting the in-laws, the trip had a few sags. Debbie, as we now called her, after just two days of travel, got addicted to the motion of the car. At night, when we would stop at a motel, Debbie would fuss the whole night. We finally would get back into the car, drive till she fell asleep, and pull off at a rest stop and sleep until she woke up again. On the third night, we stopped in Tonapah, Nevada, which was snowy and cold. Wayne went to find out where to get boiled water for formula. The lady in the motel office gave him three glass jars of just boiled water. Well by the time he got them up to our room, his fingers where burned. Then, I sent him out to get us dinner while I bathed and fed Debbie. He came back with steak sandwiches and french fries, which looked scrumptious, but no silverware. We felt like we were back in medieval times, eating with our hands. That was the last time we went through the town of Tonapah.

We arrived in the state of Washington at our destination a week and a day before our scheduled flight. Wayne took the dog over to transportation to arrange for her flight and was able to get her on the plane going out that day. They asked Wayne if he wanted to fly out the next day since the dog was already on her way. Exactly one week to the day earlier than originally scheduled, but on the same flight number, we were to leave on from the lower forty-eight states to travel to our new home for the next three years: Fort Richardson, Alaska. On arrival, we were put on the list for housing on the post, which was going to take a month or two. Our dog was waiting for us when we got there; however, it took us a month to get our car. We located a furnished one-bedroom apartment in Anchorage, Alaska that we could rent on a monthly basis and moved in. Deborah was a good baby and very content if she was fed, changed, loved, cuddled, and played with a lot. She loved her baths, and even at four months old, enjoyed splashing water all over the kitchen counters. A week after we got to Anchorage, which was the civilian town outside of the post, I was making dinner, and Debbie was in her infant seat watching me and cooing. I was expecting Wayne home at any time for dinner. It was time for the news, so I turned the radio on the station we had found and liked when we arrived in Alaska. I was half listening and half playing with Debbie as the dinner simmered on the stove. A newsflash came on and the announcer was stating that a plane full of Army and Air Force personnel and their families was missing somewhere between McCord Air Force Base and Elmendorf Air Force Base in Anchorage. The plane had apparently dropped off the radar screen, and the tower had lost all communications with them. Search planes were being mobilized to locate flight 3567. When they gave the flight number, I absolutely froze. The announcer gave the same flight number we would have been on if we hadn't gotten to Washington a week early to make arrangements for Cocoa, our dog. God's protecting hand was upon us even then, and we both felt, upon hearing the news, that but by the grace of God we would have been on that plane. Well, this story went on for months as they search every mile of the frozen terrain of the flight pattern for that plane. There was no indication that they were having any problems, the reports said. The plane and all aboard just dropped off the radar screen with no trace. To this day in 2004, they still have never found any wreckage of the plane or any of the people who were passengers.

From that day on, we appreciated our family and lives just a little bit differently than we had before. We realized that there was no guarantee that we would be here the next minute, day, month, or year. We all know this, but until you actually see the means for your life to have ended, it doesn't sink in as reality.

We waited three months for quarters and moved onto post into an eight-family unit in the month of June. We had a unit in the middle of the eight-family building that was three bedrooms and a bath upstairs, living room, dining room, and kitchen on the first floor, and a full basement. All the other units were the same. Home at last!

Deborah grew into a cute, little toddler. She was never prone to temper tantrums, and she learned quickly what was acceptable and what was not. The word no was learned but not always followed unless enforced by her mom or dad. She loved to play in her playpen with full view of the whole downstairs. The playpen was mesh with each side capable of being lowered. I used to leave one side down, and this allowed her to crawl in and out to get her toys. I would place her in the playpen with sides up when I was cooking.

One day, I was cooking a roast for dinner and left it simmering on the stove. I was in the living room with Debbie as she played in her playpen with the side facing out to the room in the down position. I went into the kitchen just to turn the roast. As I did, the roast slipped off the fork causing a splattering of grease. I jumped back and there was Debbie, standing next to the stove, looking up at me. As I jumped clear, the grease landed on her face and she began to scream. I picked her up, and acting totally out of instinct, ran cold water on her face nearly drowning her in the process. I took a clean, white towel and blotted her face being careful not to rub hard, which would have disturbed her skin. I retrieved the soft margarine from the refrigerator and coated her whole face. Just then, Wayne came home, and we rushed her to the hospital emergency room. When things like this happen, it makes you feel like the worst parent in the world. She was crying, I was crying, and Wayne was helpless once he got us to the emergency room. The doctors cleaned the butter off her face and examined the burns. The burns were first and second degree. The doctors placed ice packs on her face for a couple of hours, and then gave us a salve to coat her face with three times a day. Three weeks later, we went back to the doctors. Debbie's face had healed without any scars, and the doctors claimed it was my running cold water on her immediately, which stopped the grease from continuing to burn her. Up in Alaska, the tap water was ice cold as it came out of the facet, so it not only flushed the grease, it cooled down the skin instantly.

In December 1963, Deborah's first birthday was a big affair for the adults. How much Debbie realized it was her birthday was incidental to the joy of a mother throwing the partly. Friends and children where all there as Debbie got herself completely covered with chocolate cake because she was allowed to feed herself for the first time. Her fingers never stopped digging into the cake and all that smooth feeling icing. It was shortly after that day that Wayne and I decided that we would try for our second child. We didn't want to have them too far apart. Wayne, being an only child, definitely did not want just one, and my sister and I were four and a half years apart, which was just too far apart for any real companionship until we got older. By the end of February, there was no doubt that I was pregnant again. I went to the doctor to confirm and was told that the due date was October 20, 1964.

On Good Friday, 1964, Anchorage, Alaska had a huge earthquake registering 8.4 on the Richter scale. It happened around dinnertime, and Wayne had just gotten home from work. We were going out that night to a party at the Officer's Club, so we were feeding Debbie at the dining room table. Behind her high chair stood a seven foot tall china cabinet, which had a cut glass, crystal decanter full of bourbon sitting on the very top of it. When the tremors started, we didn't get too excited as we had them all the time. They soon sounded like a kettledrum, which was accompanied by a shaking. Well, as we sat there, they started to become more intense, and the sound increased to the point of 100 kettledrums or louder. Our quarters started to shake extremely fast, but it felt like it was also rocking from side to side against the way it was shaking.

Wayne yelled we needed to get out of the house at the same time as he pulled Debbie out of her high chair without stopping to pull the tray out. It was a good thing he did, because no sooner had he cleared Debbie from her high chair than the decanter of bourbon came crashing down to the exact spot the top of her head had been. Again, God spared her serious harm! We rushed out of the house, and Wayne instructed us to get into the car, which was a station wagon at the time, and our dog, Cocoa, jump into the back. We buckled our safety belts, and Wayne made sure both the hand and emergency break were on, plus he had his foot on the brake pedal. The car heaved and shook until we thought the very teeth in our mouths were going to shake loose. Debbie was in her car seat and did not seem to be unnerved by the quake. However, Cocoa was very nervous and was never the same after that. When the quake stopped, the car had literally moved back into the street about six feet from where it had originally been parked. Cocoa was a wreck by the time we got her out of the car, and until the day she died, she would go crazy whenever we drove on gravel roads as it sounded a lot like the noise of the quake, only much quieter. Debbie, on the other hand, seemed totally unmoved by the whole thing. As we entered the house, we surveyed the damage. At the top of the basement stairs was a series of pantry shelves where I stored can goods, among other things. Molasses was one of the items on the shelf along with flour, sugar, salt, and other dry food items. The molasses had fallen down the stairs, spilling its contents all the way down into the basement. Flour and sugar followed making a very sticky mess indeed. The kitchen was pretty secure. The rest of the first floor had pictures on the floor, and one of the big, oil paintings had fallen on the top of our entertainment center leaving a huge dent. Bourbon was all over the dining room, leaving a smell that took us over a year to get completely out of that area. Upstairs, Debbie's crib had literally walked its way across the room, ending up on the opposite side. Other than that, we were very fortunate. Wayne was called out on alert immediately, and Debbie and I didn't see him for four days as he and his troops secured the downtown area of Anchorage. Debbie had survived, at age one year and four months old, one of the century's biggest earthquakes. It was amazing to see the pictures that were taken of downtown Anchorage. Streets had just dropped about eight to fifteen feet below where they were originally located. Out by the seaport, there was a fairly expensive area of houses. These homes literally tumbled end over end down the slopes, some ending up in the water. Reports of the damage came in all that week and the death tolls kept rising. A doctor and his family were watching TV in another city, and their house split open through the middle. The opening swallowed up their two children sitting on the floor right in front of them. They just disappeared before their eyes, as he and his wife had no time to react. Ft. Richardson and the Elmendorf Air Base were built on a gravel base so it would ride out an earthquake because the gravel would move easier than the frozen earth. Except for messes, there were very few structural damages on the Army Post or the Air Force Base. A week later, the aftershocks came, and after reading of all the deaths and damages the quake had done, I was in a panic to protect Debbie and myself. The extreme fear I felt almost caused me to lose the baby I was carrying. I was more scared during the aftershocks, because by then, I had seen and heard about the devastation that the state of Alaska was in from the main quake. The calming effect of having to keep Debbie calm, and Wayne reassuring me, helped me to stabilize my system so I could carry the baby full term. Again, God's hand of mercy was with us.

For the next six months, Debbie continued to grow and so did I. During the summers, one of our favorite weekend outings was to go camping. Debbie loved going camping. She would try and catch the birds and the flying insects by waddling after them. While we were fishing, she played in the fish chest full of fish we had already caught. She was very patient when she watched daddy cleaning the fish, although she did not like it when he would cut their heads off. Wayne made us stop camping when I was seven and a half months pregnant with Ray, as he could no longer zip the sleeping bag closed over my tummy. After Ray was born, we needed a little more room, so we purchase a fifteen foot camper and camped in that until the children were in their teens and their interests changed.

In the early part of October, my parents, who had retired to Texas, came up to Alaska to help us with Debbie when I went into labor. On my dad's birthday, October 12, 1964, in the middle of a snowstorm, I went into labor, and on the way to Elmendorf Air Force Base Hospital, Wayne almost hit a moose standing in the middle of the road. We had about eight inches of snow on the ground by that time of year because once it started snowing it just kept piling up, as it did not melt off until late spring. He was able to skid around the moose and made it to the hospital in time. I gave birth to a baby boy and named him Raymond Wayne Stephens after our two dads. Raymond was a beautiful baby, all pink and rosy, and had big blue eyes. He looked a lot like Debbie when she was born, as neither looked like newborns. Three days later, we brought Debbie's brother home. Things never were the same for Debbie. She loved her brother and was such a big help taking care of him. She and Ray were twenty-two months apart, which proved to be great as they were growing up. My dad was delighted Ray was born on his birthday and kidded Debbie about taking his present home with him. Debbie refused to allow grandpa to take her baby brother anywhere and was quite relieved to see him leave without Ray.

My folks left to go home and life returned to a normal routine. Alaska was a unique place to live. In the winter months, it would not get light until around 10 AM and by 2:30 PM it was dark again. Back in the states, I was used to fixing dinner when it got dark. So that first year in Alaska, I ruined more dinners than I care to mention. But after we had been there awhile, we adjusted to all the differences.

One cold winter morning, after changing Ray's diaper, I went downstairs to where I had left Debbie playing in the playpen. Debbie was nowhere to be found. I searched all three floors of the house, and even though the front door was closed, I looked outside as a last resort before calling Wayne. There she was, out in the cold, wearing only her sleeper pajamas, playing with my neighbor's Labrador Retriever. Although it was twenty degrees below zero, she did not seem the least bit cold. I brought her inside and gave her a warm bath to ward off any sickness. When Wayne came home that night, we put locks high on the inside of the doors to insure that she could not escape like that again without my knowing.

When summer came, the temperature usually got up to about sixty degrees, which by the second summer felt like ninety degrees to us. Since the sun never sets during the summer months, in order for Debbie and Ray to sleep, we would place aluminum foil on their windows to make the bedroom dark. Debbie loved the summer months, the weather was so great she'd never want to come inside. In the winter she never got to go out and play due to the extreme cold. It was hard keeping track of the time in the summer and often we didn't. I had a harness that I put Debbie in when we went for walks. It was a regular baby harness with a strap for me to hold onto her with. Sometimes, when

I couldn't be outside and Debbie wanted to be, I would put her in her baby harness and hook her to the dog leash outside. There were no fenced yards on post, so it was the only way I could contain Debbie while she was playing. She loved it. All her toys were right there for her to play with, and it solved the problem for me when I had to be inside for a moment with Ray. One day, I was outside with Debbie when Ray woke up from his nap in his carriage. I took him inside to change his diaper, and while I was gone Debbie had a visitor. Rebel, our neighbor's Lab, came to visit her and licked Debbie's face to her delight. Before I could react, Rebel lifted his leg and proceeded to pee all over her. I was horrified, but she thought it was great fun. Needless to say that ended that day's outing and took us immediately to bath time.

At night, we would always close the drapes to help keep the house warmer in the winter. One morning, I walked into the living room to find Debbie talking away while she looked through the opening in the drapes. As I was standing there watching her, I heard a knocking on the window in front of her. I opened the drapes to discover who she was having a conversation with; a large bull moose was standing on our porch. His antlers were so enormous that they would hit the window when he turned his head. Debbie was just delighted with her new friend. It was quite sometime before the moose decided to leave our porch, and Debbie stayed there talking with him through the glass the whole time he was on the porch.

While we were in Alaska, Wayne had changed his branch of service from Infantry to Military Police. Consequently, when it was time to leave, he got orders for Ft. Gordon, Georgia to attend the Army Military Police School. We left Alaska in the month of April of 1966. We decided to drive the Alcan Highway which at that time was 1200 miles of gravel road. We still had the fifteen foot Alhoa travel trailer that we pulled behind a Chevy Impala Super Sport car. It took six days at thirty mph to travel into Canada and another four days' travel to enter the United States through Great Falls, Montana. It was a trip of a lifetime. Debbie was three and a half and Ray was one and a half years old. We had them in seatbelt harnesses that worked out really well. They could sit, stand, and move from side to side a little better than kids today can in car seats; although, I will admit they were not as safe. Again, the Lord watched out for us. For being so young, we were happy that both children were so good on that long trip. We stopped off in Illinois to see the Stephens' (Wayne's parents) and then traveled down to Texas to see the Beggs' (my parents). My parents lived on Lake Buchanan, and we really relaxed from our long trip. Debbie learned to swim and fish, falling in love with the water. After spending two weeks in Texas, we drove on to Ft. Gordon, Georgia. On arrival, we bought a house, as there were no homes to rent. So we settled down for a year while Wayne went to school. At the end of school, Wayne got orders to Vietnam, so we sold our house in Georgia and rented a house outside Ft. Hood in Kileen, as it was the closest army post to my parents and my sister whose family was stationed there. Debbie started nursery school and loved school from that time on. She was an above average student throughout her years of schooling.

While Wayne was in Vietnam, he took R&R in Hawaii, and I joined him, leaving the children with my parents. I also left our pregnant German Shepherd, Cocoa, behind. With Debbie's help, my dad helped delivered Cocoa's first litter, which was only one pup. It was a very large puppy, and it was unfortunately stillborn. This was a hard experience that Debbie had to go through. Both she and her grandfather buried the pup in the backyard as she insisted in taking part in this. When I got home, she had to explain everything that had happened while I was gone. This was the best thing for her because she got to work through all her feelings as she told me about the event. I was proud of the wonderful job she did explaining everything to me, not leaving out one detail. We rebred Cocoa and had a successful delivery of six beautiful puppies. Both our folks took a puppy, shipping a male pup back to Wayne's folks by plane and sending a female home with my dad to Buchanan Dam. Debbie was in seventh heaven with six puppies to play with for at least an eight-week period before we got all of them placed in good homes. It was a good experience for Debbie to have after the unfortunate one with the first pregnancy.

While Wayne was in Vietnam, the hardest part was trying to explain where daddy was. It got even harder when he called from Vietnam via Mars Station. She could not understand why she could hear her daddy but could not see him. She was only seven at the time.

On return from Vietnam, Wayne was on orders to the Presidio in San Francisco, CA. We packed up our household, said goodbye to the folks, and traveled to Illinois to see Wayne's parents before we headed to California. We rented a house in Daly City, CA, which was about twenty minutes south of the Golden Gate Bridge just east of I-5. We were on a hill overlooking the bay of San Francisco with the San Franscisco Airport below us in the foreground. The planes would fly right over our house to make their decent to the runway. When we were fogged in, which was most of the time, the planes sounded so close we thought of turning on the coffee, as we were sure they would be coming into our living room for a landing. The fog usually lifted by early afternoon, which allowed the children and me to go to the beach. Whenever it was sunny, and the kids came home from school, we would pack up the Volkswagen convertible and head to the beach. Debbie and Ray learned to play in the waves and just had a wonderful time.

San Francisco Zoo was the first one Debbie had been to. She was wide-eyed in wonder at seeing the animals in real life that she'd only seen on the TV show Wild Kingdom and Disney programs. The petting zoo was her favorite even when the goat tried to eat her coat.

Another first for Debbie while in San Francisco was Fisherman's Wharf. My Aunt Madeleine came to spend a couple of days with us, and one day, we all went to the Wharf. I will never forget Debbie's delight at seeing all the fish laid out on the sidewalk tables. The smells we experienced and the live lobsters in their tanks along the sidewalk fascinated us all. But for the young, it was delight beyond belief for their small, bright eyes.

Wayne got out of the Army in May of 1969, and we moved back to Illinois where Wayne started his banking career and where the children grew up. We started out in Alsip, then Beverly, which was a suburb of Chicago. During this time, Debbie grew into a fine young lady.

When we move into our home in Beverly, Debbie was eleven years old. She was very responsible and watched Ray for us much better than any of our older babysitters had done. So, we gave her the job when I went back to work full time to watch her brother for us. Wayne worked three blocks away and I was fifteen minutes from them. She did a wonderful job for us and was very responsible, never hesitating to call us with a question. As I think back, and if I had it to do over again, I would have not gone back to work after Ray entered first grade. Not because Debbie didn't do a great job, because she did, but because the job really was mine to do.

One year, on our anniversary, Debbie decided she would fix us dinner. She laid out the best silverware and china, made ice tea, and served it in our crystal stemware. She fixed steaks, mashed potatoes and gravy, and green peas. Everything was served to us under candlelights. She and Ray ate with us, and as we started to eat, Wayne got the funniest expression on his face. I couldn't guess what was wrong, but it only lasted an instant and then he covered it up. Well, when I started to eat the mashed potatoes I realized what had caused his distress. The potatoes were instant and very salty. The steak and peas were great, but we suffered eating every bite of the potatoes. We never said a word to her as she had done a wonderful job and had just put way too much salt into the potatoes.

About two weeks later, she was helping me make dinner, and I decided to ask her to fix instant mashed potatoes. In doing so, I was hoping to find out why she had put so much salt in them for our anniversary dinner. She got out the measuring cup from the cabinet and started to mix a cup of salt into the potatoes when the box only called for a teaspoon. I corrected her on the measurement and asked her to look at the box directions again. When she did, she turned and said to me, "That is why the potatoes were so salty the other night. Didn't you guys think they were salty?" I told her I thought they were a little salty but didn't pay much attention as the whole meal was so good. After that, she would study a recipe closely before proceeding with the mixing of ingredients. One thing about Debbie, she always learned from her mistakes and rarely did she repeat them.

We finally moved out of Beverly to Oak Lawn, Illinois, where I worked at the First National Bank of Oak Lawn. Debbie was just turning twelve, and she started to roller skate as a fun activity to do with her friends. As she got used to skating, she became interested in skating lessons. One night, after talking to us, she went to see the pro about taking lessons from him. After their conversation, we discussed the possibility of her taking lessons. We made a decision, after finding out the cost, that this was something we would like to provide for her. Thus in June 1974, Debbie embarked on a new direction for her life. Free Style Roller skating was what she had decided on for her sport and after six months it was apparent that she was quite good. In 1976, she entered her first competition. Boy, what a wreck that makes out of the parents. When she would trip or fall during her performance, we wished it had happen to us.

As a family, we had many fun hours around our above ground pool. The kids were constantly entertaining their friends and Debbie, on several occasions, brought her entire skating club over for a pool party.

On December 23, 1975, Debbie turned thirteen years old. So ends Debbie's first twelve years. During this time, she was a very good girl giving us very little reason to lose sleep. She had gotten good grades up to this point in school and always kept us informed of where she was and what she was doing.

There had been a normal sibling rivalry between her and her brother Ray but nothing out of the ordinary.

On most occasions, they really enjoyed each other's company, and the older Ray got, the better friends they became.

WE WERE PROUD OF DEBBIE AND HOW SHE GREW HER FIRST 12 YEARS!

Wayne came back into the hospital room, bringing me back to the present time. With him were our Pastor and his family. Wayne had contacted the children to be back to the hospital at 5 PM that evening. We informed the head nurse, who by this time was stationed out side Debbie's door, that we would let them take Debbie off the respirator at that time after everyone had said their goodbyes to Debbie. Our Pastor and family stayed with us the rest of the afternoon and comforted us through prayer and their presence. Our Pastor reminded us that before Debbie went on the respirator she told him that if Jesus wanted to take her home, she was ready to go. There was such a peace in Debbie's voice when she said that, it brought us all such comfort.

CHAPTER TWO
OUR YOUNG LADY

How could this be happening! We just brought her into the hospital last Sunday, Oct 27th. She had called us as we were getting ready to go to church and asked us to take her to the emergency room when we got out of church. I remember the previous Thursday she was still not feeling well after fighting a cold and congestion for two weeks. She was planning on staying home and in bed during the weekend to rest and get better. When she called on Sunday she complained about not being able to sleep Saturday night due to having problems with catching her breath. Wayne didn't wait for church to be over. He immediately went to the house and took her to the hospital. As soon as my Sunday school class I taught was over, I joined them at the hospital. Brad and Kathie were up in Chicago with their dad. It seems like this was all happening to someone else and we were living in their lives. As I looked over to the hospital bed that held Debbie, I cried out to God to heal her and leave her on earth for awhile longer. But then I told the Lord that I wanted His will done for Debbie, not my will. He could see the future, and He knew what was best for her. I drifted back to 1974 and Oak Lawn, Illinois—

As Debbie and Ray got older, their roles totally changed. Debbie was neat and Ray was messy until their high school days, and then it was reversed. The same thing happened to their handling of money. Debbie was a saver, and Ray spent it as soon as his hands got a hold of it. But when they were older, Ray became the saver and Debbie the spender.

We liked to go to Texas on vacations because my mom and dad lived on Buchanan Dam Lake in Texas, and we would spend the whole time fishing and swimming. My dad taught both the kids how to water-ski and how to handle a boat when pulling a skier. We had a lot of good family fun on the lake, as well as going out to the German-American Restaurant for dinner with the children. Ever since the children were small, we always took them to nice places for dinner. Our friends use to criticize us for taking them to such expensive places like the restaurant at the top of the John Hancock building in Chicago, but Debbie and Ray knew from a very young age how to dress and act in any type restaurant because we taught them by experience. We told our friends who criticized us that it was good training. However, people we did not know in the restaurant would stop and compliment us on their behavior like Ray helping his sister with her chair.

We all loved vacationing in Texas at my folk's home on the lake. Even our dog, Cocoa, loved to swim and chase sticks in and out of the water. On a couple of our summers with my folks, we had the pleasure of my sister being in the area because her husband had two tours in Vietnam. During these times, our children were finally able to get to know each other. We loved to go exploring around the hill country of Texas and often took the kids to San Marcos and the Inner Space Caverns for fun things to do.

Karen and Debbie got to know one another and became close friends during these vacations. One summer, we spent a week of vacation down in Arizona after my sister's husband got re-stationed at Fort Huachuca, Arizona. They bought a great house with an in-ground pool and plenty of room for us all. The kids loved the pool and getting to know their cousins better. We took them on day trips to see the Bisbee Turquoise Mine, Nogales, and into Mexico across from Douglas, Arizona border. A grand time was had by all on these summer vacations with our children. We all preferred warm weather and sun bathing, so we usually headed south or out to Oceanside, California. Debbie especially loved to get a suntan to show off her great figure. She looked terrific in a tan, as we all did, and it was healthy for us. When Karen got married, we flew Debbie down to Arizona to be in the wedding. She had a marvelous time. Debbie was around seventeen at the time of the wedding and still did not have a steady boyfriend. So she just relaxed and loved being with her aunt and family. Debbie loved mingling with the wedding guests and dancing at the reception. When she got back to Illinois, she filled us in with all the wonderful stories of the great time she had. Debbie always shared everything with us, especially girl talk with me. By this time, I was not only her mother but her best friend.

Debbie really didn't date a lot. She was very mature for her age both in mind and body. She had boy friends but mostly older than her as she found boys her age did not think as she did nor did they have the same interests. The boys she did date were usually just someone to have fun with. She continued to do well in school and bring home good grades, sometimes it seemed, without studying.

Dinnertime was always our family time. No matter what anyone's schedule was like, we all tried to make dinnertime at home a priority. When they came home from school, they were too busy with homework, playing with their friends, or doing after-school activities or chores. But at dinnertime, the TV was off, and we would sit for hours around the dinner table just discussing everything. The children knew they could tell us anything, including off-colored jokes they might have heard. We would listen to what ever they told us and then tell them one of three things: either they should never tell that story again, that was a story for the same sex, or that it could be told while in mixed company. It seemed to satisfy them just to be able to tell the story once after they had heard it. If we told them not to tell it again, they never felt the need too. We discussed all sorts of topics and problems and we always counseled them on what they should not be doing and what they should. We told them that there was nothing they couldn't discuss with us, but that once we discussed it and made a ruling, they had to abide by that ruling.

Debbie also wanted to take organ lessons as we had always had an organ in our home from the time they were young because I played. Ray was not interested in playing any kind of instrument, not even a guitar. We set up the lessons with a teacher that did not turn out the way we wanted at all. The teacher kept insisting that

Debbie learn piano first and that turned her completely off. She didn't want to play the piano, she told us and if the teacher wouldn't teach her the organ then she would forget the whole thing. We tried to find another teacher, but by the time we did, she was much to busy in dealing with horses.

As Debbie got older, she never had many sleep-overs or dated a lot. When she did go out, she was always home at the designated time. We always encouraged our children to have their friends over to our house for several reasons. Wayne was never allowed to have friends home when he was growing up, and he always said that he missed that opportunity. The second reason was that we knew where they were and what they were doing. They never had them over, however, unless one of us was at home--this was one of those non-negotiable rules and they abided by it.

During the time Debbie was growing up, I cannot remember when she was ever grounded for doing something she wasn't supposed to. Debbie was a good girl and never really caused us much cause for concern. Her brother was the one who seemed to always be getting into trouble. He always lovingly called Debbie, "Miss goodie two shoes." We thought he was just upset because he always got in trouble more than Debbie ever did. Ray's problem was he could never lie to us without giving himself away. He always tried to explain too much where, on the other hand, Debbie had a knack for making you trust her and really said very little. Little did we know that there were some things such things as pot or alcohol Debbie was trying, but she never really liked it, so it never became a problem for her. Thinking back, I remember Debbie having nightmares in the middle of the night terrified of about frogs. She would wake up screaming that the frogs were going to hurt her. I never knew where she got this from because as a youngster she played with frogs. But once, Ray told us about her experimenting with things we didn't approve of, I think maybe that had something to do with the nightmares. When she was fully awake, she knew they were nothing to fear. Wayne remembers walking into her room one time, and it was totally covered with flies.

We could not figure out how they got into the house as all the windows had screens on them. We never did find out how they got in but we managed to kill all of them.

Debbie was getting quite good in her skating by now. She switched to a new instructor that was in Chicago Heights, Illinois. We would go with her to skating lessons every week and watch the lessons. It took forty-five minutes to drive from where we lived to get to the rink, so we started to talk about moving to the Chicago Heights area. On one of our trips out to the rink, we spotted a "For Sale" sign on a great house just down from the rink. After discussing the prospect of buying it, we put our house in Oak Lawn up for sale and signed a contingent purchase agreement on the new house. Wayne has always claimed we bought that house because of Debbie's skating, which was a factor, but there were other reasons for purchasing a house in that area. Wayne had left Mt. Greenwood Bank, which was near to Oak Lawn for a position of Vice President and Cashier at Homewood Flossmoor

Community Bank. His new position was nearer to the Chicago Heights house, and it had plenty of space for the kids to grow.

Once we moved into the new house, the children began spending a lot of time at the skating rink. Debbie was in skating competitions, and those were very stressful times for me. Every time she fell or made a mistake we wished it was us out there hurting. As a family, we skated for fun, and Wayne and I even took some dance lesson. In 1976, Debbie's instructor entered her in the Illinois States Competition for Freestyle Roller Skating. We were all so nervous. Freestyle roller skating was gaining in popularity but still didn't equal the popularity of figure skating on ice. Debbie placed fourth in the Ladies Free Style Competition. We were so proud of her even if it made us all a nervous wreck. The intensity of a competition got Debbie thinking that this was not something she wanted to do much longer. She like the competition, but she was getting more interested in her horse that we had bought her shortly after we moved to the new house. Ray's horse was an

Appaloosa, and Debbie's was a Quarter Horse. They had fun taking care of them and riding in the country side around our house and the rink. Debbie tried her hand at training her horse and was quite good. She had a way with handling him that amazed both her dad and me. Ray was good with his also; however, he just wanted to go riding.

We eventually went into the horse business and bought a little ranch in Crete, Illinois and sold our house in Chicago Heights. Debbie hung up her skates as far as competition and just did it for fun. After a family discussion with our accountant telling us we needed a tax shelter and talking with the children, we decided to turn having horses into a business. We decided to show and raise Arabian horses. We called our ranch Lindy's Acres. Debbie worked our horses training them, and Ray was our barn manager, taking care of the cleanliness of the barn and helping Wayne. Debbie took care of the horses. Now, looking back, it was a silly venture for us to take on, but we didn't know the Lord in a personal way, and we went the way of the world getting deeper and deeper into debt while creating a tax shelter. We purchased an Arabian brood mare of excellent quality and showmanship. Debbie started working for an Arabian breeder and trainer to learn more about how to train and ride with a show presence. She showed their horses, as well as ours, and did quite well. She was also very instrumental with helping us determine the stallion we wanted to breed our mare to. For the rest of Debbie's school years, we had the horse business, which kept her and Ray busy and out of trouble.

I remember a time I was called out of town on business for the bank I worked for. Our mare was about to deliver her first foal, and I really didn't want to go. But I knew the rest of the family was more capable than I was and that the mare was in good hands. We had an intercom system between the house and barn so we could hear what was about to happen. Usually, the barn would go dead silent (even though we had twelve other horses) when the birth was happening. The mare did foal while I was away with lots of complications.

The foal was doing well. They were up all night giving the foal blood transfusions. The veterinarian stayed with them through the night. I kept in constant contact with the family as the foal was still in a lot of trouble. We finally lost the foal but not because of the care it got. The mare rejected the foal as soon as it was born. They have a way of knowing when the newborn is not right. Debbie, Wayne, Ray, and the vet bottle feed the foal for forty-eight hours but finally lost the battle. It was heartbreaking for all of us. We were told that this sometimes happens with the first pregnancy, but our mare had had other foals with no problem. We buried the foal in the yard behind the barn. A year later, the same mare successfully gave birth to a beautiful colt. What a joy that was to have a baby on the ranch. He was not to be our last either, and we were grateful for that. It was a very expensive but exciting time and learning experience for us all.

I remember at one of the horseshows, Debbie was not only showing horses, but they also had to be cared for and gotten ready each time they went into the ring, which took a lot of time. She was so busy at this one show that she never changed her contact lenses which really needed to be taken out every night. By the third day, she decided she needed to tend to the contact lenses, but one was stuck tight to her eye and it was very painful. We rushed her to the emergency room, and they worked for over an hour before they finally got her lens off her eye. She had to wear a patch over that eye for the rest of the week, but that didn't stop her from performing her duties for the trainer. Debbie actually went into a surrey class with the trainer's stallion and won. We just watched in amazement as she displayed her strength to overcome this obstacle.

At another show, Wayne remembers her telling us about the night she slept in the stalls with the horses because it saved time. It was a short two day show and the hotel that the trainer booked them into was too far from the show grounds. She awoke that night with a young girl and one of the ranch hands making out in the next stall to hers. That was the last time she spent the night with the horses. From then on, the trainers let Debbie stay in their trailer next to the barn and she was much happier.

There were a few things Debbie did not care for when it came to the care of the horses. They used to twitch a horse's nose to get him to cooperate when they needed to do things that the horse didn't like or understand. Twitching the horse entailed pinching the nose between a vice like instrument. One such time was when the horseshoer came to the barn to fix a shoe on one of the stallions. The shoer wanted Debbie to twitch the stallion but she refused telling the man that it wasn't necessary. The man was very skeptical but finally did the work with Debbie holding the stallion. Debbie calmly talked with a soothing voice to the horse the whole time. The horse never budged but stood perfectly still with his head against Debbie's chest. She certainly had a way with animals, and she was good at her job. During this period, she started smoking. She thought we didn't know because she always had incense going in her room to mask the smell of smoke. I don't think I really caught on but Wayne knew. We were smoking

Lynn Stephens

cigarettes ourselves at that time, so we really could not come down too hard on her. There were things she was doing that we never found out about until years after her death when Ray informed us during a time we were going down memory lane as a family.

I remember Debbie's first car. It was a Cougar, and I didn't like it because I felt the steering wasn't right. There was too much play in the wheel, and Wayne agreed with me. Neither one of us liked to drive it, but Debbie was proud of that car and kept it until we finally sold her our mustang with the sunroof which she also loved. We felt better about her driving it verses the Cougar.

During her senior year in high school, she worked part time for a local bank. She really liked working in the same field that her dad and I were in. She started to enjoy getting dressed up and going to work at the bank rather than wearing jeans and mucking the stalls. (Mucking the stalls is a phrase used for cleaning the stalls). Her grades were still good in her senior year, but she really didn't participate in any school activities. She still preferred older men, and because of this, never went to her senior class trip or prom. I think we failed her in that way by letting her grow up too quickly.

After high school graduation, Debbie was doing so well at the bank that they asked her to work full time for them. She was well liked by both peers at the bank and the customers. She had never discussed wanting to go to college and had always said she wanted to be a wife and mother first and foremost. Therefore, she did not want us to spend money when she just wanted to take care of a family. She was very good at her job and found herself advancing to supervisor and was in charge of a remote bank location.

Working for the bank was good for Debbie, but it also influenced her thinking. None of us knew the Lord. Wayne continued to change banks for advancement opportunities and salary increases. Debbie learned from this, as well as from listening to her customers tell their stories; these customers were very wealthy and high rollers. Debbie wanted a secure lifestyle and dreamed of being married to someone on his way to success. Until the end of her life, I did not realize how much her yearning for a worldly successful life influenced her decisions.

During her time at the bank, she met her first husband, who was a customer of the bank. Debbie was nineteen when they started to date. He was twenty-six years old and had been divorced once, which we never knew until they were engaged to be married. They were attracted to each other from the start, and it was hard for us to interfere, although we did caution her on dating someone seven years her senior. Once we got to know him and took into consideration that Debbie was mature for her age, we were vocally against them dating. Ray was a junior in high school when they started dating.

After several months of dating, they fell deeply in love. They seemed to be everything the other had ever wanted. I remember a picture I took of them, each of them staring into the other's eyes. The love was so thick you could cut it with a knife. Debbie loved his large family and enjoyed being with them all at family gatherings.

I sat down in the hospital next to her bed and prayed that God would heal her or peacefully take her home to be with Him. It was 2 PM on Wednesday the 30th of October. In three hours, the family would be back, and they would take her off the respirator. Oh how I prayed instant healing would come at that moment, giving her back to us for a while longer.

Wayne was taking care of some friends and family in the ICU waiting room. I picked up my Bible and just started to read the 23rd Psalm aloud to Debbie and for my benefit. We were both walking through the Valley of Death, and we needed to feel the Lord with us. Wayne finally returned to Debbie's room with friends who wanted to see Debbie and pray for us all. What a comfort to have praying friends and family.

CHAPTER THREE
MOTHER AND WIFE

I continued to read the Bible to Debbie after Wayne took the friends back to the waiting room. I felt so guilty at the fact that I could not have helped Debbie avoid this situation with her health. As a mother, I felt I had failed her so many times. On the other hand, she made her own choices, and I was not with her twenty-four hours a day. She always wanted to talk, but never once mentioned she had a problem with stress or alcohol. I saw the signs that something was wrong as she was losing too much weight to the point of being a walking skeleton. Why did her husband not see what was happening and help her? I thought to myself. I had to ask God to forgive me for thinking that way, for her husband probably tried. Debbie had asked us not to notify her husband (this was her second marriage), when we checked her in to the hospital. She was very frightened of him, but she never told us why. Brad, her son, seemed to know something, but this was not the time to question him. There was more going on than I knew, and that definitely had to be left with the Lord, although I wanted to know deep down. If God chose not to heal her, I was going to lose a daughter, and I knew only two-thirds of the reason why. Oh, how we wished things could have been different and that we did not have to suffer the consequences for our choices. God will forgive us all as he had Debbie, but that did not release her from the effect of her choices. It did not take the damage out of her body that the alcohol and stress had done. Where was her husband? We did not know! Both of the telephone numbers we had were disconnected. Maybe it is a blessing for the children that we couldn't get a hold of him. Maybe we did not try hard enough because deep down we knew the children were hurting and would be upset to see him. Oh Lord, forgive us for any wrongdoing on our part.

I went back in my mind to Debbie's first real love with a young man who was much older. She was so sure of what she wanted...

Debbie did not date anyone else from the time she met Tom. They went everywhere together and enjoyed the same activities. Tom came from a very large family who were always having gatherings that the whole family would attend. They all seemed to like and accept Debbie from the start. The mother and father, however, were somewhat concerned because of the age difference. However, like all of us, they were hoping that their relationship would work out for the best. As time progressed, we all got accustomed to seeing the two of them together.

One night, around 10:30 PM, Debbie and Tom walked in the back door. They wanted to talk to Wayne and me together. Wayne was getting ready for bed, so I went and got him. Once we were both down in the kitchen, we asked them what they wanted to talk to us about. Neither of them would come all the way into the kitchen. Instead, they stood by the back door and leaned against the stove, which was there as you entered the house. Debbie told us they wanted to take their relationship to the next level, but she wanted our permission before she gave herself to him. We both kind of took a deep breath and sat down. This is not what we were expecting. What a place to be in, thinking you are a Christian but having never received or had a relationship with the Lord. I did not know what to say, and I am sure that Wayne was trying to keep his temper in check. This is not something, as parents, that we wanted to deal with. It would have been better if they had just done it. Well, not really for her, but for us. We talked with them for awhile trying to get Debbie to change her desire. I do not remember how long we talked, but in the end, we did not change their minds. We finally asked Debbie, "If we said, 'Absolutely not,' (which we should have) would you do it anyway?" Debbie knew we were not happy about this circumstance. "Yes," she said, "but I wanted you to know upfront that we had talked about it and decided that we loved each other enough to take our relationship to the next stage." I wish that my mind had been clear enough to tell them the next stage was marriage, but I did not think about it at that time. We really could not prevent this except to say we did not give our consent and we were very disappointed.

A couple of months later, Tom asked for Debbie's hand in marriage. From then on, we all were very involved with the wedding plans. This was May, and they set the wedding date for November 13, 1982. We planned a big, sit-down wedding that cost a fortune, having all the thrills and goodies attached to it after the style of wedding that was expected. Talk about having to keep up with the Jones'—financial woes.

During the time of planning the wedding, I got sick and had to have major surgery, which had at least a six weeks' recuperation period at home. The surgery went well, and during the recovery time at home, I read a book someone had given me titled, *The Late Great Planet Earth* by Hal Lindsey. I was very fascinated by this fiction story. I knew it was about the book of Revelations from the Bible. One day, while I was outside reading the book, my neighbor, Joyce, came over to see how I was doing. She saw the book and asked me how I liked it. I told her I was very interested in what Lindsey had written. She told me she had some of his tapes on the book of Revelations where he actually explained what God was telling us in the Bible. My mother, who was staying with us at the time to help with the family while I recovered, and I listened to the tapes every chance we got with great interest. At the end of each tape, he would give an alter call for those who wanted to accept Jesus into their life. Now I had gone to a mainline denominational church all my life, and no one ever told me the necessity for me to repent and ask Jesus to forgive me and come into my heart and save me. Absolutely no one! By the end of the fourth cassette tape, I was on my knees begging God to forgive me. I saw clearly I was a sinner and needed salvation. That night, when Wayne came home, I told him what had happened. I think he thought I had finally lost all my marbles. When he gave me a drink, which we had every night, I took one slip and it tasted bad. From that time on, I never had hard liquor again, and I can count on one hand how many glasses of wine I have had since being saved. The desire to drink was gone. No one told me that I should not drink because I was now a Christian. It just was not something that I desired to do anymore. Wayne now had to drink alone, and he did not like it.

A week after being saved, we drove my mother back home to Arizona in our mini-motorhome. I spent the entire trip down to Arizona sitting in the back of the motorhome, at the dining room table, reading the Bible. I found several Bibles in the house, including the white one I had carried on my wedding day. I kept pestering Wayne, who was driving, when I read something that just astounded me. I think he thought I was preaching to him, but I could not get over how I had been in church all my life and no one had told me what I was now reading. I do not think that I ever had a preacher encourage me to study the Bible on my own. The denomination that I attended had their own version of the Scriptures in the back of the hymnbooks, so we never even brought a Bible to church. I read the entire New Testament on that trip and could not get enough of it. It felt like I had a teacher inside of me telling me what the Word meant. I had no idea it was the Spirit of the living God, who was now living inside me, until we returned home. I remember when I was a young girl, picking up the Bible on many occasions, but I soon got discouraged as I could not understand what it was saying to me. A few days after we got home, I went over to bring the Revelation tapes back to my neighbor. While having coffee with her, I told her what had happened to me and she got so excited. She told me she was a Christian and had been praying for the neighbors across the street from her for their salvation. She never dreamed I would be the one to be saved, and she invited me to her church Sunday. I dragged Wayne with me, as I wanted so much for him to experience salvation. It was a little, country Church of God church, and the pastor was on fire for the Lord. When he gave the alter call, I literally ran forward, and I am sure I embarrassed Wayne. I knew, from reading the Bible, I had to make a public confession. I never in my life have felt such love and release of all my burdens. He forgave me and opened my eyes to see the world through Him. The peace and joy where beyond description, and I floated home. Wayne could not get over the change in me.

A few months later, Wayne accepted Jesus into his life at a night service and started studying the Word for himself. We realized that we had a dilemma that we were going to have to deal with regarding Debbie's wedding. The wedding was in a few months, and we were having an open bar at the reception. This was not what we now wanted to do, but how were we going to discuss this with Debbie and her soon-to-be husband as they both drank and so did their friends and family? We prayed and prayed about it and received counsel from our pastor as well as from our neighbor, Joyce and her husband, Eulish. We prayed more about it and decided we needed to change the open bar reception. We told the kids we were going to allow an open bar for one hour before dinner. We would then shut it down, and it would become a cash bar. We would also serve one glass of champaign for the toast. It wasn't the best solution, but the kids were okay with it. It was only a deterrent, and we prayed that God would protect all who were attending the wedding. God granted us His favor as no one who was driving that night drank too much. We were so thankful, grateful to Him, and relieved.

The wedding was beautiful. Debbie chose to wear my wedding gown with a few design changes. It was a one-of-a-kind dress from New York's Fashion House made entirely of Chantilly lace from Italy. It had a cathedral train, and she looked beautiful in it. She had a new veil made for it, which was a simple cylinder of white roses with the veil coming off the cylinder. It was so simple but so elegant. I still think of her today looking like she did that day. She is now with our Lord and Savior, and she most assuredly looks more beautiful than I ever saw her.

The wedding was a candlelight ceremony with dozens of white roses and satin ribbons. We had invited over 500 people and most of them showed up at the reception. The church service had about 300 people watching them say their vows. My heart was bursting with faith and hope for their future. Tom had become a part of our family, and we loved him as if he was our own son, and still do to this day. The reception following was a gala event and all were having a wonderful time. Debbie and her husband had picked a great band that played modern and not so modern music. All who attended the wedding were happy with one song or another. Tom had to cancel their honeymoon plans due to work but promised Debbie that they would go on one as soon as the business deal he was working on completed. I could tell she was disappointed, not so much with not having a honeymoon, but with the fact it seemed her husband's business was his first concern.

They decided to start a family right away, and she became pregnant shortly after they were married with our first grandchild. We gave her a baby shower at our ranch in Crete, IL. We had it outside under a rented tent, and everyone brought great gifts and had a wonderful time. I remember Debbie was quite big at the time of the shower. She never complained, however, even though it was a very hot day. She looked wonderful when she was pregnant. There is just something about a pregnant woman.

The next year, on September 1, 1983, their first child was born. A beautiful, baby boy and they named him Bradley Thomas. Debbie was a wonderful mother, and she loved her baby so much. She was thankful to have a child to occupy her time as she hardly ever saw Tom. He was so busy starting a new business that it took him away from Debbie during the week, and on many weekends, unless they had a family function to attend. Debbie enjoyed the family functions. Tom had four other brothers and two sisters so there were plenty of children and people to talk too. She loved being married, a wife, and a mother. Occasionally, I would detect an unhappy undertone, but I kept it to myself. I waited until she was ready to share it with me. I tried so hard not to be an interfering mother or mother-in-law. Maybe I should have been more concerned but Debbie always put on a good front.

Debbie got pregnant with their second child but had a miscarriage when she was in her second month. She was so depressed after that happened that she started to let her dad and me in on some of the unhappiness she was feeling. Apparently, she and Tom rarely had supper together. She would eat alone and save his dinner for when he did make it home. Debbie sometimes felt she was the mother of his children, a housekeeper, and cook, but not much else. Well, this started a two-year period of discussions with her on how to hold on to her marriage. Divorce was never an option in my family, and now, as a Christian, we knew this was not in God's will. This was something I wanted to help her avoid. They were married under God and were a unit. Even though we were not Christians at the time, it was not how Wayne and I were raised. There was a commitment they had made to each other, and she needed to have patience in working through the difficulties.

It was shortly after Brad was born that Wayne lost his job at the bank where he was working. The efficiency experts the bank hired to find ways to cut cost came back with the biggest cost being salaries. Cutting salaries was exactly what happened, and since Wayne was one of the newest hired officers, he was one of the first to be let go. I was not happy that my husband lost his job, but it was a relief. He had felt the Lord trying to get him to look elsewhere as this job was stressing him out and he was working late hours. The bank was also involved in un-Christian ethics, which bothered Wayne, and was probably why the Lord wanted to move him on. So, as usual, when we do not obey and want to serve the Lord, He steps in. Wayne went through six months of trying to find a job. Before every interview, he would tell the Lord, if the job was not for him, then close the door. If it was the right job, then open the door wide so that he would know the Lord was in it. We had only been Christians for two years when this happened, and it definitely brought a growth in our walk, showing us how to rely upon the Lord. After six months, we traveled to Arizona to visit my mother and sister who lived in Tucson. After our vacation was over, Wayne and I decided he should stay in Tucson and explore the job opportunities. He kept the motorhome and lived in it while I flew back to my job in Chicago.

After several weeks, Wayne secured a job with a new bank as a consultant with the promise to stay on as an officer once the bank opened. It was a joyful time to know that God wanted us to move to warmer weather, as this was the desire of our hearts. I gave notice at my job and put the house up for sale. They allowed me to continue working until the house sold. Once the bank in Tucson opened, they did not hire Wayne as they had promised, so, once again, he was out of work. Wayne needed me, and I felt the Lord telling me to go for a visit. I took a long weekend and flew back to Arizona. We sat in the motorhome and prayed, discussed, and prayed some more. We felt that the Lord was telling us to move to Tucson. We had to make the decision to step out in faith and trust Him. Being apart was not working for either one of us, nor did we feel it was God's choice for us. We made the decision that I would go back to Chicago and prepare to move in thirty days, giving final notice to work. If the house did not sell, we would leave it with a real estate person. As it turned out, Debbie and Tom approached us to buy the ranch if we would carry the financing for them. We agreed and they took over making our mortgage payments and signed a contract with them that our lawyer drew up.

I was off, the car packed, the furniture on its way, and the dog beside me. It was hard leaving Debbie, as I knew she was still in turmoil, but maybe it would be best if I were not so accessible to her. Maybe it would help her grow and rely on her own strength. When we arrived in Tucson, we settled in a nice apartment. Wayne found a job, and we were beginning life all over again. A fresh start was good for us, and the Lord was faithful through it all.

The next two years I spent talking on the phone weekly with Debbie. She would call miserable about how her marriage was not working out. I tried to give her wisdom from God, telling her to hang on as things would pass and get better. She got pregnant with their third child, and this seemed to calm things to a degree. I remember when they came down to visit before Kathie was born, she was delighted to be pregnant, and her husband seemed to be very attentive toward her again. On Oct 23, 1985, Katherine Anne was born, and I flew up to be with her during the birth. Tom was there in the beginning, and once the baby was born, he was rarely at the hospital. His company, again, drawing him away, or so we thought.

Kathie was beautiful and such a happy baby. Debbie was so content with her children but not happy about never seeing her husband. We talked about how hard it was for the family when forming a new business. I told her to have patience and be there when her husband needed her. I only stayed two weeks and then had to return to Arizona. During those two weeks, I tried so hard to encourage her to get involved with a Christian church in Homewood, where they lived. I told her that the Lord would help her if she would only give this situation over to Him. Well, she rejected that idea as she was not ready to commit to the Lord. Oh, how foolish we are in all our own wisdom when truth is only of the Lord. However, we do all have to discover that fact for ourselves.

Another year of telephone conversations went by. We went up to see them during that year and I remember, one day, I was standing by the fence watching the horses run and play in the corral of our ranch, now theirs. Tom approached and stood at the fence with me. I had never talked to him about his marriage or divulged anything Debbie had confided to me. I had been observing some things since being there and made my concerns known to him about his family. He promised me he had everything under control and that all would be fine. I suggested that unless he started spending more time with his family, they would travel down a road of hardship, and possibly, the end of a marriage. He again told me that would not happen. He was unable to see how miserable his wife was, or if he did see it, he did not want to admit that things were not as they should be. Maybe he felt that by not doing something it would all correct itself.

After we had returned home, Debbie and Tom's problems seemed to escalate. There was such desperation in her voice when we would talk to her. The few times we would talk to Tom, he seemed equally frustrated. The following year, Debbie and Tom filed for divorce. They had tried to talk through their problems, but they were never resolved. She was devastated.

Debbie wanted to take the children and move to Arizona to be near us. Tom wanted to give us back the house. We prayed hard about this, and then talked to our attorney. He told us that the decision was ours. We had a binding contract but felt it was God's will to have the house returned to us. We placed the house on the market, and when it sold, we made a slight profit. God is so good.

I flew up to Illinois and drove back to Arizona with Debbie and the children. On the trip back to Arizona, she filled me in on so many things that had happened which Wayne and I were not aware of. It was then that it became clear why everything she tried to do to save the marriage did not work. This was so sad! I kept seeing the way they stared into each other's eyes the night they announced their engagement. They were so in love. Without the Lord being placed at the head of your home, Satan can lie, steal, and destroy every hope one has for the future.

We moved furniture around and made our dining room into a bedroom for her and the children as I had my mother living with me at the time. She got a good job at a bank and was liked by her coworkers and customers. I could see that she was still hurting over the end of her marriage. When she went out with friends, she drank too much and sometimes stayed out too long for a work night. We did not allow liquor in our home and smoking was out because my mother was on oxygen, and we did not want the influence in our home. She felt in order to handle the stress of her failed marriage, she would stop by a club on the way home from work with coworkers. She knew the children were fine.

We helped Debbie buy a home for her and the children in our area so she was still close. I noticed when I visited her that she always had a drink by her chair. It was a clear liquid, so I never was sure what it contained, although I had my suspicions. She never appeared to be under the influence, nor did I smell any alcohol on her breath. She was a grown woman, and I hesitated to be an interfering mother.

About a year after she had moved into her home, Debbie met her second husband, Charles, at one of these after work stops. He was an entrepreneur and had family money that helped him live when deals where slow to materialize. He would find and put together the project with the moneyman. He would get a percentage of the total project, which was an enormous sum, since the deals where in the millions. They started to date, and they had a good time. He seemed like a nice man and treated the children with love.

Since I worked out of our home, I was delighted to be able to watch the children during the daytime. Debbie allowed us to take them to church with us, and they started to hear things of the Lord and His love for them. The Lord helped the children to deal with the divorce of their parents in a way that really astounded me. Grandpa was both father and grandpa to them for a time, which gave them that father figure they needed. We all loved these children and they felt the love in our home. They called my mother "GG" (great grandma) and loved going down to her room and cheering her up with hugs and kisses.

During this same period, Debbie was also dating a nice man who worked for an airline company as a steward. Both men seemed to adore her and the children. Although still being disappointed over her marriage failure, she started to come out of the sadness that seemed to always be under the surface of her life. We prayed constantly that the Lord would save Debbie. Neither of these men were Christians, although they thought they were. After some time of dating both men, she decided she needed to date one or the other. Both were talking to her about a relationship commitment and a decision needed to be made because complications where happening even though they both knew about one another. She finally left the relationship she had with the steward and concentrated on her relationship with Charles. Many times I questioned in my mind the wisdom of her decision, but I kept my mouth quiet as I knew I did not have wisdom to help her with this decision.

Their relationship grew into love. He decided that it would be better to move to California because that is where his deals seemed to be. She and the children moved out shortly after he found an apartment for them not far from his. The children wanted to be baptized before they left for California. The children met with our pastor to discuss their baptism, and Debbie was behind their discussion. After their meeting, the pastor was sure they were both ready to make this next step after their salvation, which happened four months prior. Debbie found a job as a branch manager of a bank in Malibu that sat right on Pacific Coast Highway. She was finally happy. The children loved being in California, the beach, and the weather. They were always having picnics on the beach and swimming. During the summer before our grandchildren started school, Debbie and Charles discussed the school situation where they were living and it decided was the best. They made two major decisions that summer that took their relationship to a new level. One was to move to Malibu, where the schools were excellent. And secondly, since he had just closed a big project, they decided to rent a house overlooking the ocean on the cliffs in Pacific Palisades and move in together. We were not happy that this was happening before marriage. We were not fooled into thinking that they might as well live together since he was always at her place and spending the night.

Once they moved into the house, we went to see them the next summer. They all seemed to be quite content, and the children were thriving in their new surroundings. The house was gorgeous and had a great floor plan with the children finally having their own room. Debbie knew we were not happy with her setting up housekeeping without the marriage so we did not have to voice this to her. We tried to love them all and prayed that this would end in a happy marriage.

The following year, Debbie called us with the happy news that they were going to be married on November 13. They were hoping that we could come to the wedding. They were going to have the wedding at home overlooking the ocean, and the children were going to be a part of the wedding. She talked about an hour that night telling us all the plans they had already discussed. It had been along time since I had heard her so happy. I lifted them all up in prayer. If I remember correctly, my prayer was something like, "Lord make this all turn out alright for them as a family."

The children's father, although he was not much of phone person, did manage to break away from his work a few times each year to see the children. Debbie was always uneasy when they were visiting him. He had closed his business and moved to Texas, close to the New Mexico border. He used to come get them and take them home with him. The children always seemed to be glad to return home...

November arrived and we all drove out to California for the wedding. It was beautiful, and again, Debbie made a stunning bride. Our granddaughter was in a dress similar to her mother's, and our grandson was in a tuxedo. The children were calling him dad and all seemed the perfect picture. We had a great time. After the wedding ceremony, we finally got our first look at her ring. It was beautiful. White gold, with three enormous diamonds set in the band. She told us that it belonged to his family for many years. They went to Hawaii on their honeymoon, and the children went back to school. They had a nanny who was a young woman that the children adored. We headed for home happy that Debbie had found happiness at last for her and the children.

There was peace from California for over nine months, and then we started to detect certain things from my daughter when she called. They had split the bills in half, and Debbie was buying groceries and paying the utility bills out of her pay; while Charles was taking care of rent payments and other unexpected expenses.

It seemed that Charles was not a saver as she was. When they had plenty of funds, he would not put away for when the deals were slow to come to completion. Charles started to sell things to meet the rent and other expenses when money was slow to come in. This was stressing Debbie out. She had always been one to plan for a rainy day and he was not. They did not discover their differences in money matters until after they were married.

Finally, we got a call. They had decided to move back to Arizona and were going to buy a house in Scottsdale. We, of course, were delighted that they were going to live closer to us. It was a two hour drive to Scottsdale from our home in Tucson, all on good roads. The day came and they leased a home. It was beautiful and far too expensive if they were having money troubles, but they assured us that all was well. Debbie's husband even convinced her not to work outside the home but to be his business manager for his entrepreneur business. The first trip up to see them was a pleasant weekend and all seemed to be going well for them. Wayne, however, felt something was wrong but could not put his finger on the problem. The children were happy; her husband showed great love for Debbie and the children. Why then, as we went home that weekend feeling happy, did peace evade us? Something was definitely malfunctioning.

I walked over to Debbie's bedside and wished we could start all over again to raise her. This time it would be different, Lord, because you would be involved from the beginning. However, by the grace of God, I might be laying were Debbie was today. The Lord had entered my marriage in time to be the adhesive glue. We think we are so wise with our own understanding, yet we realize, once we are born again by the grace of God, that our thinking was as filthy rags.

I looked at my watch. It was three in the afternoon, and in two hours, we would pull her life support from her. Tears started to run down my cheeks. As I took my daughters hand in mine, I prayed again for healing. I so wanted to be able to give her back to her family, but then, that was not in my power to do, but only in God's. "Lord," I prayed, "give me your grace and power to get through the next minute, hour, day, and weeks." I thought of the children and continued, "Give them the strength that they will need and show them how to trust and rest in you, Lord."

I placed Debbie's hand back on the bed and she never moved. Was she already gone? I asked myself. Should we wake her up before they pull the plug to say goodbye? Lord, help us have your wisdom in all these matters.

CHAPTER FOUR
STRESS AND HEALTH

I watched as her chest moved up and down with the respirator. The machine was breathing for her, and I wondered how long after we stopped the machine her chest would cease to move. Debbie was only thirty-three years old, and it seemed impossible that this was happening. Then I thought, Why not, Lord, you are not a respecter of persons. It can happen to anyone. Lord help us to reach out to her children when they return to the hospital in two hours. Give us Your wisdom to see this through with love and gentleness. I will never take the place of their mother, Lord, but let them know that I love them deeply and will be there for them when they need me.

I realized that not only are we losing our daughter, but also, the children will no longer live near us. They will be in Illinois with their dad for always. Oh, my heart is truly grieving for us all. How would we ever get through such a loss if we did not have the Father, Son, and Spirit to help us in this very hour of need? Tears again slid down my cheeks and I was overwhelmed with sorrow. Wayne came into the room, and knelt down in front of me, and held me tight. When he pulled away, I could see the tears pooling in his eyes. How was he going to get through this? He cannot go to a funeral of an acquaintance without being affected, how he is going to get through his daughter's memorial service? I took his hand in mind and prayed for the Lord to give him strength and to comfort us all.

As we sat in silence, I drifted back in thought to coming home after that first visit to Scottsdale, knowing something was wrong, but not knowing what it was.

They had been living in Scottsdale about four months when we finally went to see them. We wanted to go sooner but we were being patient and allowing them the luxury of being able to unpack and get settled. As we talked frequently with Debbie and her family, things seemed to be moving along for them all. Her husband, Charles, was wheeling and dealing; the children liked their community and school. Both of them always did make friends easily, and there was never a problem getting them involved. Debbie was being a stay-at-home mom and loving that part. She was also handling all of her husband's correspondence and office matters in his office at the house. She sounded like she missed banking but was enjoying what she was doing. She once told me that it was so nice to be home when the children came in from school. They were so anxious to tell her all about their day. When she was working, they would forget half of what they wanted to tell her by the time she came home from work.

During the first visit, we were able to feel the vibes of the family better than over the phone. Her husband was always working or waiting on a deal to come through. This worried us a little since Debbie was not working, and in his profession, money would be tight at times. Thank God we taught Debbie how to plan well and save.

When we pulled up that first day in front of the house they were leasing, we were astonished at not only the neighborhood but also the expense of the house. Debbie told us later that it cost a quarter of a million dollars. They felt justified in spending that since the home was also an office and clients would be coming and going. Back then, a quarter of a million was a lot of money to spend on a home. It was beautiful and very functional. It was a two story home with three bedrooms, three baths, living room with fireplace, dining room, kitchen with all the gadgets, family room with another fireplace, office off the living room, swimming pool and Jacuzzi, plus a two and a half car garage. The outside was southwestern in design, as were all the homes in this newly constructed area.

The children loved having a pool in their backyard. I think that Sierra, the wolf dog they had, loved the pool also. In fact, she was in it as much as the children were. Sometimes we would look outside and there was Sierra swimming all alone.

On our second visit, a couple of months later, we started to see things unravel. The children seem to be uptight, especially Brad. Debbie was losing weight and seemed to be under a lot of stress. I remember, one morning while we were all sitting around talking over coffee having a great time, her husband was upstairs taking his shower. He called down to Debbie to come up to their bedroom. She was gone for about twenty minutes before they both came downstairs. He was very demanding of Debbie to meet all his needs.

Her husband had a big deal come in and it involved a lot of money. He decided that they could afford to get another house because their year's lease was coming up, and the property owner was giving them difficulty about the lease renewal. We never really understood all that was happening, but they made the decision to buy a home that was twice as much as the original one they had planned to buy. It was gorgeous, but I knew in my heart that this was going to make it difficult for them financially. Wayne tried to make sense of why they needed another home. This one seemed more than they needed, but her husband insisted they needed the other house to entertain their clients.

They bought the house and moved in. We tried not to interfere. They were adults and knew what they could afford, I prayed. It was about six months after this that we got a call from Debbie. They were completely out of money, and she had no food to feed the kids. When I asked her what happen to all the money they had gotten from the deal that closed a while back, she told me Charles had spent it all. She tried to have him put half away for times like these, but he just kept putting her off until it was too late. At the time, I was working for Pathway to Freedom, a drug rehab women's ministry, and we had access to the food bank. I got permission to get extra food for Debbie when I went to get food for the ministry home where the women lived. The next week, Wayne and I took the food up to Debbie and the family. While there, we sat Debbie down to find out just how bad things were. She was drinking a glass of what we though was water, and when she needed a refill, I was going to get up and get it for her, but she insisted on doing it herself. From that time on, I noticed she would always get her own water and never was without a glass at her side. I was glad she was drinking so much water, but I still did not like the weight loss. When we asked, she told us that it was a lot of stress not having money to even give the children for lunch. The bills were backing up, and it was a repeat of California, when they had been evicted from their home in Brentwood. She wanted to return to work to help out, but her husband needed her to stay home to work for him. This was great that he wanted her involved, but his company was not paying either one of them a salary. Between the constant demand on her body and her time, with no money to feed her family, stress was taking a toll on her health. She also worried about them not having any medical insurance. This really alarmed Wayne and me because we knew that a medical crisis could put them in a financial crisis. Her husband had his real estate license, and we tried to encourage him to go back into real estate to bring in the money they needed. Apparently, he had been very successful; he had even opened his own firm and became a broker. However, he insisted the big deal was right around the corner.

We took food to them about four more times, and once she came down and to get the food we had gotten from the food bank. They lived like this for a few more years, either being in the money, or not having any. I was so sad to see them all going through these tough times. I remember praying for the Lord to use these times to get their attention. They were living for the world and trying to keep up with the Jones'. As much as they loved one another, we could see this lifestyle was taking its toll on Debbie.

When Wayne's mom passed away in May of 1994, they came down for the memorial service. When Debbie walked into the church that day, I wanted to cry. She was so thin and looked horrible. I mentioned that I thought she had lost too much weight to her husband, but he seemed unconcerned. Our whole family was in shock at the way she looked. I tried to talk to her, and she admitted she had lost some weight, but did not admit to how bad she looked. I did not know what to do, so I prayed. I had no wisdom in how to handle this situation. However, it was not until our visit in July of 1995 that I saw before me a walking skeleton. It was this visit that I also found out that she had not been drinking water all these months but vodka. It was then I realized that she not only had stress problem but one of alcohol too. We tried again to talk with her and her husband. We wanted Debbie to consider a rehab to overcome this, but they would not here of it. No money! She was of age so there was nothing I could do but to suggest that she look into those programs that helped people in her status. However, she fell through the crack of every rehabilitation program because of their lifestyle. The second house was even more than the first, and it was hard for them to prove their need of financial assistance. There were rehabs out there, but they were very expensive. I suggested that they sell her wedding ring. It had to be worth quite a bit of money. It was worth enough for rehab, but Debbie told me it had already been hocked years ago to get them debt free out of California.

After trying repeatedly to get them to sell the house and most of what was in it to change their financial situation, I realized an awful truth. Debbie was not her husband's first priority. He loved her but not enough to start over again.

We got a frantic call from her husband in the middle of the night in March of 1996. Debbie was passing a dark substance, and it was all over their white carpet on the way to the bathroom. He did not know what to do. We told him to take her to the hospital immediately or call 911. He asked us to come get her because he could not deal with her anymore. We had come to their rescue so many times it was hard to tell him this was his responsibility to take care of Debbie. He needed to put his pride behind him, go apply for Access Health Insurance for her, and get her to the hospital. This was my baby, and I wanted so much to go get her and the children, but they had made choices that resulted in her condition, and he needed to be a man.

Two weeks later, we got a call from Debbie from Scottsdale Memorial Hospital. She was a patient with internal bleeding, and they were going to do a procedure on her. The doctors took x-rays, and one of her major arteries had a slit in it. They were going to have to go in through her neck with a shunt to slide down the inside of this artery to the place that was torn. This would stop the bleeding. Her kidneys also showed damage from both the stress and the drinking. She was in a dangerous situation. The doctors told her that the procedure they wanted to do was very dangerous, and she had a 50/50 chance of coming through it with her life. They were going to do the procedure within the hour. She wanted us to pray with her and we did. We wanted to go up immediately, but it was a two hour drive. We thought we couldn't see her before the procedure, so it was better that we waited until we got the results. We asked to speak to her husband, but he had left to go on a business trip before it was known she was having this procedure. The neighbor woman had the children.

I never prayed so hard in my life for God to deliver her and not take her until she found Him and had salvation. I think I prayed until Wayne called the nurses station. We found out that she had come through it without any problems. We left a message for her that we were on our way. We packed a bag and left right away. By the time we got up to Scottsdale, we knew the children were still in school, so we went right to the hospital. She was in her room but looked awful. She had a slight yellowish tint to her skin, which was from the alcohol. Her doctor told her that she would be in the hospital for two weeks, and that if she ever had another drink, it would kill her. Well if that won't wake a person up nothing will. We stayed up in Scottsdale for a few days until her husband came home and could be there for the children. Brad was twelve and Kathie was ten at the time.

The day Debbie was being released from the hospital, I was so happy for her and the family. She had not had a drink for three weeks, her coloring was back to normal, which gave us all hope that her weight would improve.

She called me when they finally got home. I was little worried because I knew what time they were releasing her from the hospital. She told us her husband picked her up at the hospital with the children and on the way home insisted they stop at a bar to celebrate. Debbie tried to talk him out of this as she could not have a drink and should not be in a place that served liquor. He would not listen; he told her she needed to take charge and have will power not to be tempted. He also refused to throw out the liquor in the house. He was, to say the least, not at all willing to change his style of living for her. Some people have a funny way of showing love for one another. In fact, when I hung up from that phone call, I realized that without the Lord in your life, love was just on the surface. It was not a deep down, lasting forever love like the Lord's.

From that time on things went down the hill very fast. He was verbally and physically abusive to her and even threatened her with a knife he kept in the office. We did not find this out until later. The end of March, only home two weeks, she called us frightened, confused, and stressing again. We talked for quite awhile about the Lord, how she needed to turn her life over to Him. He would give her direction and protection for her life, giving her the boldness to do what was right. After about an hour on the phone, I could hear the desperation in her voice and asked her if she wanted to accept Jesus into her life, and to my surprise, she said yes. We prayed with her the sinner's prayer and welcomed her into the family of God. As soon as we were done, I remember her words. After she controlled the crying she said, "If I had known it was this glorious, I would have done it sixteen years ago when you first talked to me about the Lord." We were so happy for her. We knew that this did not change her situation but now she had the Holy Spirit living within her to help and guide her through life. I told her to get the Bible down from wherever she had it and start reading the book of John.

Charles continued to be abusive to her, and she became more and more frightened of him. She started to put some weight back on, and he complained that she was getting fat. When I heard that, I realized why she never saw herself as we did. He liked her skinny. One thing that still puzzles me today is why she let him have such control over her life. She was such a self-willed child and teenager while growing up, she was the last one I thought would find herself in this kind of situation. She allowed him to buy her clothes and told her what to wear and when to wear it. He was jealous of her, although with her working at home, she did not have much chance to meet anyone for him to be worried about. As scared of him as she was becoming, she still loved him. Her love for him was keeping her from breaking free of the dominion he had over her. We do not blame him, because she made choices and was reaping the consequences of some of her bad choices.

The month of April was a really bad time for her. Money was still tight, and he was not home much due to his business. She found signs that maybe there was someone else in his life but never wanted to confront him. She learned to be calm and pray. Thank God she had the Lord to see her through this. I wanted to be there all the time but my job and Wayne would not allow it. He was right of course. I would have made things worse for her. My presence would have told him she was talking openly to us and that could have really put her in a bad circumstance with him. I also learned to commit her to prayer more than normal. We still did not know all that was going on in their home, and we tried so hard to not judge anyone. This was the hardest thing that I ever had to go through. I prayed for her husband to find the Lord and to see the harm he had contributed to in regards to her health. He said he loved her all the time to us but would never change his lifestyle for her or the children.

Through this all, we were starting to see in Brad's eyes especially, the stress the children were starting to feel. Things must have been happening that they heard or saw. I found out years later that they saw Charles shove their mom in a not so gentle way while they were in the same room. This was very disturbing for them, but they kept it all inside of them.

The Saturday before Mother's Day, she called me and told me that while her husband was out of town, she was leaving him. She and the children wanted to come down to Tucson. She did not want a divorce but needed to get away to get control over her situation as he was not helping her at all. He was still keeping liquor in the house, and it was very hard for her not to succumb to the temptation, taking in the fact of the friction in the home.

Her cousin, Randy, was going to help her move down to Tucson, and she asked if we could let her and the children stay in the house we had for sale until it was sold. We told her absolutely, in fact, we decided that we would take it off the market and let her stay in it as long as she and the children needed it. She left a note telling her husband that she needed to move away from him until she could totally get better. She did not want a divorce but needed time to sort through things and get her health back. She only brought items that belonged to her, our family, or the children, such as their furniture, and left everything else in the house.

On Mother's Day 1996, we went over to the house after church and waited for them to get there. They arrived about one in the afternoon. I was so glad to see her but was surprised to see that she was still so thin. The children and the dog were with her and all looked happy to be free of a stressful situation.

Now that she was in Tucson with us, we learned more of the things that were happening in the family from her and the children. I am not going to go into who did what as that is not my intent of this book. Besides, I would not break any confidence that either Debbie or the children might have told me. It always takes two or more to create a bad situation. Yes, sometimes one is more responsible, but we all make choices, and we need to accept certain consequences from those. Debbie was concerned for the children's well being and for her recovery. That says enough.

The children were getting ready to go for their summer stay with their dad in Chicago, and Debbie was getting signed up for all the services that could help them eat, sleep, and have medical coverage, something they did not have up in Scottsdale. She had to legally separate from her husband in order to be eligible for any aid programs, and this she did. Debbie said she loved her husband, but needed to get herself turned around in order to better deal with the lifestyle that she had not known before getting married. She wanted to give her husband some breathing room. If he did not have to feed, cloth them, and take care of their expenses, maybe he could get financially back on his feet.

Debbie loved our pastor and was in church with us every time the doors were opened, which thrilled her dad and me. It was an answer to our prayers. The children were in church on regular basis either with us or their Dad. We prayed for them every day from the time they were born.

Debbie prayed about how she could turn her life around. She finally admitted she had always wanted to get a nursing degree, and our community college had a program that was available to her. She got government assistance to help with the finances and got a job working for one of the professors at the college. She loved her classes and her job, and we could see a change start to occur in her life. She was still struggling, but she continued to get back up and continue down a new road the Lord had opened up for her.

When she moved down, she brought one of the vehicles with her as they had two in the family. Shortly after she had gotten settled, Charles came and took the car from her as he wanted to sell the sports car he had been driving. This left her with no transportation other than public transportation. She learned to get around on the public transportation, and when I did not need my car, she used it. Many times I just let her drive me to work and then come pick me up at night. I felt better knowing that if something happened during the night that she would have transportation.

As the summer progressed, the children where doing well with their dad and having a great time as they did whenever they went there, reacquainting themselves with their dad's side of the family. They missed Debbie and their dog, Sierra, but loved being with their cousins. They were now ten and twelve years of age, so they could pretty much fend for themselves. Debbie had done a wonderful job with their upbringing. They were loving and kind, always considerate, and willing to help when needed.

During the summer, Debbie gradually gained her weight back. Her body started to fill out to the point her bones were no longer visible. Her hair started to get the luster and highlights back that had dulled during her sickness. Her stress was losing its claim on her body and on her face.

She loved her job with the professor at Pima Community College which helped to support the family. Debbie was enjoying her studies and doing quite well. Her courses kept her busy with the amount of homework she had and between that, going to school, and working, the summer went fast.

About two weeks before the children were due back home, they called Debbie and asked if they could spend the next year with their dad. Debbie was disappointed they did not want to come back to Tucson, but understood their feelings. She loved them and would miss them but knew that it was time for them to reunite with their Dad in more than a summer situation. They really didn't know their father's side of the family that well. So, she gave her permission for them to remain in Chicago. In the next few weeks, she wondered if she had done the right thing. She was going to miss them an awful lot and it would not be the same with them not with her. But then, she realized that she needed to concentrate on getting herself back up to peek condition, and that with the children in Chicago, she might be able to accomplish this better. Even though she was at peace with them being gone, not a day went by that she did not talk about them. "They were the only things," she would say, "that I have accomplished that turned out okay." They were a blessing from God for all of us. Both sides of the family loved them for who they had become.

After taking a few courses during summer school, Debbie started with the fall semester. She loved going to school and her grades were in the top ten percent of her class, which she was proud of having accomplished. She remained in church with us. Every time there was a study or service, Debbie was right beside us. We watched her grow in the Lord, and as she got stronger in Him, we saw a new glow about her.

One night, at a women's meeting, she gave her testimony on how the Lord had saved her and brought her to Tucson. During her talk, I suspected that something was wrong. She seemed to be out of sync with herself. After the meeting, I found out that she felt like she was coming down with a cold. She needed to be very careful because her system was still trying to recover from her last hospitalization. The date was October 17, 1996. From that day on, Debbie started to slide backward in her recovery.

A couple of days later we talked and she still was feeling poorly. She told me that a bad virus had been going around the office and school. At that time, there was a virus that they had no antidote for that had killed some seniors and young babies during the beginning of the fall seasons. I prayed it was not the same virus. She fought this for two weeks as she continued to go to school and work. Thursday, October twenty-fourth, after picking me up at work, she asked me to drive her home and take the car. She had the next four days off, and she was planning on going to bed and resting. We told her we would not call her, not wanting to wake her if she was sleeping. She agreed to call us if she needed anything. I dropped her off at the house and went home, praying all the way.

Sunday morning, as we were getting dressed for church, Debbie called. She was not doing well at all. She told me that she had not slept all night because she could not breathe and felt if she fell asleep she would not wake up. Debbie wanted us to come pick her up after church and take her to the emergency room. We told her that her dad would come up right then and take her. I would follow as soon as I finished teaching my Sunday school class.

On my way to the hospital, I remember praying for the Lord to be with her and us through this troubled time. Never in my wildest dreams did I think this was fatal. I knew Debbie was in trouble but thought it was nothing that the doctors could not handle. When I walked into the emergency treatment room, I could see for myself that she was having a terrible time catching her breath. Wayne informed me that they were going to admit her into ICU. They needed to run tests and to start her on an IV. We stayed with her the rest of the day. That night, we left when visiting hours were over to get some rest, but we were back early on Monday morning. Around 10 AM, the doctor came in and talked with us all. Debbie's liver was failing and the blood test that they took the day before showed a large amount of alcohol in her blood. We were in shock, and Debbie was in complete denial that she had had anything to drink. Because of this, she was not eligible to be put on the list for a liver transplant. Right up to the end,

Debbie denied drinking. Her breathing was getting harder for her, and she requested that she be placed on oxygen until they could finish running their tests and also to give the antibiotics a chance to work in her system. She was getting breathing treatments every hour but nothing was clearing her lungs.

Our pastor and his wife came in around noon that day. They talked with Debbie, and the pastor encouraged her to trust in Jesus no matter what happened. We all held hands with Debbie and prayed for God's healing to come and for His grace to under girth us through this trial. When the nurses came in to place her on a respirator, they told us that once connected, she would have to communicate through other means. Just as we were leaving the room while they got her ready, Debbie grab pastor's hand and said, "Pastor, if the Lord wants to take me home, I am ready." Those are the last words we heard her speak. They were the most comforting words I could have heard at that moment. Not that I wanted her to go home to the Lord but that she was ready no matter what was in her future. The rest of the day we did all the talking and she just nodded or wrote on a pad. I read the Bible aloud to her and it gave all of us great comfort. Of course I prayed. I was a walking prayer channel for her. My mind was on God and His healing power that I knew without a doubt He had. That night, when we finally got to bed, I laid my head on my pillow and through my quiet tears, released her into His hands.

"Lord, I must trust you through this. I have no way of knowing your plans for Debbie at this time. If you take her home, you will give her the ultimate healing. But I know that your power is strong enough to heal whatever is wrong with her body and let her live here on earth a few more years. I think of her children who need her, and her dad and I will have such a void in our life without her. Please Lord, heal her. Nevertheless, Lord, your will be done, not mine."

Tuesday, October twenty-nineth, we arrived at the hospital at nine in the morning. There was already a crowd of people in the waiting room praying for

Debbie and waiting to see if they could get in to see her. One of the people from Wayne's bank ordered food to be brought in for those remaining throughout the day. Wayne and I went in to see Debbie and find out how she faired throughout the night. The doctor was in with her so we waited outside at the nurse's station until he was through. He called us in and talked with all of us. Debbie was experiencing pain, and he was putting her on a low dose of morphine to help her rest. She was still in a very unstable situation. The antibiotics were not clearing her lungs, and her system was starting to give up. We were told that the healing that had taken place over the summer was reversing itself, due to the complication caused by the infection in her lungs. The doctor told us we should notify the family that she was in very critical condition. At noon, we went out and called Tom, the children's dad, and told him that Debbie was in the ICU and very sick. We thought he needed to prepare the children of her condition as things were not looking good for her right now. We asked him to have his family pray for her and promised to keep him updated. We also tried again to find Charles, her husband, but none of the phone numbers we had available were working.

That afternoon, the nurses started to let the people come in to see Debbie in ICU two by two. This was not normal as it is usually only immediate family members who are allowed in this unit, and then, only for five minutes. All that afternoon our friends prayed for Debbie, loved her, and talked to her about the Lord. She responded as she could but sometimes was not visually aware of their presence. This gave us great comfort to have our brothers and sisters in the Lord surrounding us with their love. When we took two back, one of us would stay and fellowship with those left in the waiting room. The staff let everyone that had kept a vigil all day have their time to pray over Debbie.

The events of that afternoon spoke to me of friendship and loving each other. It also told me the staff did not think she was going to make it. Around four in the afternoon, they had increased the doses of morphine that they were giving her as the pain was increasing.

We never really saw the evidence of pain. All we saw on Debbie's face was peace. By the time we got home that night, we decided we needed to call Tom back and have him bring the children to us. We called for about an hour and got no answer on his home phone. We finally, out of desperation, called Tom's parents. They told us that Tom and the children were already on the way down to Tucson and would be arriving at two in the morning. They were planning to take a taxi right to the hospital. We called the nurses and informed them of the situation and asked if it would be alright if the children and Tom saw Debbie that early. We would be arriving around 4 AM. They assured us they would be waiting for us.

Tom's mother had given us the flight information, and we were at the airport when their flight arrived. They were anxious to get to the hospital, and we did not delay after retrieving their luggage. As we walked into the ICU, the nurses met us and took the children into the room with us following close behind. Debbie looked peaceful. The nurses had done her hair in a

French braid and they had reduced her morphine level so that she was awake and able to see the children and communicate. They stayed with her until about eight in the morning and then went to the hotel to get a few hours sleep as none of them slept on the flight down. After they left, we called Ray, Debbie's brother, and gave him an update.

It was now Wednesday, October thirtieth, and the morning went fast as there were still people wanting to bring love and prayers to Debbie. For six months, Debbie had been a part of our church, and they all loved and adored her. There were times Debbie failed, but everyone loved her and kept encouraging her to go forward with the Lord. She always regrouped and started over. I know that she was moving forward by the way she looked. If she had still be under the stress and drinking, I know she would not have gained all the weight back. Looking at her lying in that hospital bed, she was beautiful. Her body had completely recovered its shape, and although she looked terribly worn out, she had no stress lines in her face.

At one o'clock, the doctor came in and checked her for the third time that day. He took us out into the hall and told us the bad news. He told us there was nothing more they could do for her as her system was shutting down. Not only was her liver failing, but her kidneys were starting to shut down. Her lungs were not any clearer than when we brought her in, and since she requested that she not be kept alive artificially, he suggested that we take her off the respirator. After that, he could not tell us how long she would last once off the respirator. It could be seconds, hours, or days. We informed the doctor that we would called the children back to the hospital at five that afternoon, and once they saw their mom, we would allow the respirator to be removed. We called the hotel and informed Tom to bring the children back to the hospital by five that afternoon as they were going to take her off the respirator. We also called the pastor and my family who were in Tucson. We called Ray back, and he and his family left for Tucson. The rest of the afternoon, I read the Bible aloud to Debbie and prayed for God's grace to fall on us all and get us through whatever came next. I trusted God no matter what happened. Wayne was there beside me, and we tried to comfort each other. They could not bring the morphine level down enough for us to communicate with Debbie as she would have been in too much pain with all of her systems shutting down. Though she was legally separated from Charles, her husband, and Debbie had given us medical power of attorney of her health decisions, we still tried to find Charles. We were unsuccessful.

The children returned to the hospital at 4:30 PM and stayed with their mother until five, when the rest of the family arrived. Wayne and I had verbally stood over Debbie and told her what was going to happen when the children arrived. I have heard that many people who were in comas, even though hers was morphine-induced coma, state that they still could hear those talking around them. So I always stayed upbeat and informative for her to know what was happening. Shortly before five, our pastor and his family came by. We all prayed over Debbie for the last time and left the room so that the nurses could take her off the respirator. When they finished, we all went back into the room and stood around her. I was by her head on one side of the bed and Kathie, her daughter of eleven, was on the other. Wayne was next to me and Brad and his dad, Tom, were next to Wayne. At the foot of the bed was our pastor and his family. Next to Kathie were my sister, and her daughter, Karen, and her children. We watch Debbie try to breathe on her own. The breaths were not coming one right after another. The breaths were spaced too far apart, and I think in a matter of minutes her breath stopped all together. Kathie was laying her head on Debbie's chest when she stopped breathing and the monitor went flat. She screamed, "Mommy, Mommy, don't leave me!" In that instant, the monitor started up again, as if Debbie had turned at hearing her daughter's cry and was coming back. I leaned over to touch Kathie's shoulder and said, "Honey, you have to release her to Jesus, because if she stays with us, she will be very sick." Kathie never looked up or hesitated. She just whispered, "Mommy, I release you to go with Jesus." At that moment, the monitor went flat, and she was gone from us, but not forever. We will see her again.

We were numb and just going through the motions after that. The pastor and his family were the first to leave as they had a service in less than two hours. The rest of us just tried to comfort one another. We felt like we were in a dream. The children were in a state of shock. Brad was angry, and it was not until much later that we found out his reasons. We did tell him that what ever happened to make him so angry, he had to forgive. It was the only way he would get peace and be able to cope with the loss of his mother.

We left the hospital around 7:45 that evening, and Tom and the children came back to our home behind the church. As we sat down, I felt in my spirit we needed to go over to the church and be with our church family there. So Wayne and I went to the sanctuary while Tom and the children went to the youth service. As we walked into the church that night, they had just finished the Wednesday night Bible study. When they saw us, they all came around us and held us. Pastor came over and asked us what we were doing there. We answered, "Where else can we be comforted but by those who love us in the Lord?" We prayed and prayed with our brothers and sisters in Christ for about forty-five minutes. They all knew Debbie was with the Lord as the pastor had announced it that evening from the pulpit. We found out later that the same thing happened with the children. Everyone loved and prayed with them, and Tom was quite affected by the display of love for his children.

We parted that evening with plans to meet for breakfast the following day. We called the mortuary the next morning for them to pick up Debbie from the hospital. We still could not reach Charles. I think it was a blessing for the children that we were not able to reach him. We did not understand all that had happened before Debbie had come down to Tucson, but it was clear it was not good.

Deborah Anne, God's Blessing

Thursday morning, as we met for breakfast, we planned the memorial service. Tom and the children had to return to Chicago Friday afternoon. We planned to have the memorial service for Debbie Friday morning, November 1, 1996. We got a hold of all the necessary people and placed a notice in the paper. We phoned a few people to see if they would say a few words on Debbie's behalf. No one turned us down. As I prayed on who needed to be asked, the Lord placed the idea in my heart that there would be a church full of unsaved people, and this was an opportunity for them to hear about salvation through Jesus. I felt Wayne needed to say something also, but when I asked him, he said he would never get through it. Wayne asked one of the men in the church if he would read a statement from him and he agreed. So, Wayne wrote out his statement and gave it to the brother before the memorial service started. My sister's daughter, Karen, sang a few songs and did a piece with Kathie, Debbie's daughter, about a mother speaking from heaven in answer to her daughter's questions from earth. Next, Brad and our son, Ray, spoke together. Brad could only say that she was an awesome mom. I spoke for fifteen minutes on how Debbie was on fire for the Lord and shared the Gospel with those in attendance. So many others got up and told how Debbie had affected their lives. I will share some of those statements in the final chapter. We had a dinner following the service, and it was then we got to share and love all the people that thought enough of Debbie to attend. Debbie had been so kind and generous to those around her that people wanted to be with her. Once she had turned her life over to the Lord, the spirit of God enhanced her personality, and love showed through her life like a beacon.

We went home after everyone had gone from the church and we had taken the children and their dad back to the airport. We collapsed and were numb. As we were sitting on the couch, we thought to call Charles's sister to enlist her aid in trying to find him. We should have thought of this before, but it just didn't happen. Debbie's body was at the mortuary being preserved because only Charles, being her husband, was able to make those arrangements. They would let us bury her in the ground, but we knew that is not what she wanted. Only Charles could authorize her body to be cremated, and besides, he needed to be able to see her before anything happened.

Charles's sister, after trying all the phone numbers she had, called his attorney to enlist his help in finding Charles. When the attorney answered the phone, she was told that Charles was sitting across from him at his desk. Charles's sister had to break the news to him and he went into shock and despair. Heading to the bathroom, he threw up. Once he regained his composure, he talked with his sister again. She told him that we had been trying to get a hold of him for two weeks. Debbie had been very sick, succumb to her illness, and had died on October thirtieth. She told him the kids were here and that we had to go ahead with the memorial service without him because they needed to get back to school. Charles then called us. He was very angry with us. I could understand his anger. The whole problem of trying to find him, but at the same time, being concerned more for the children, had been hard on us. We told him we had tried on several occasions to find him and apologized to him for not thinking to enlist his sister's help sooner. After a very hard conversation for us, and for him, we told him he needed to go see Debbie and take care of her cremation. Months later, we found out that he had gotten Debbie cremated and had her ashes in a storage unit until he could go to the ocean and spread her ashes. We found out that he had a memorial service for her up in Scottsdale, Arizona, which was good for Charles to get some closure.

For the next two years, we saw Charles off and on. We went to lunch or dinner with him and just talked through the hurt feelings he had toward us for not trying harder to get in touch with him. We loved him and understood, but at the same time told him that he was still hard to get in contact with on the phone. Every time we tried to call him on the information he had given us, the phone, address, and even his email were not good any longer. Eventually, after two years, we seemed to have mended the relationship. Debbie loved him, and for her sake, we did not want to lose contact with him. We still have to contact him through his sister, as he is always on the go.

Two years later, we finally asked him to take Debbie's ashes out of the storage so that we could spread her ashes in the sunshine and fresh air. He agreed, and we went to Ft. Huachuca, Arizona and spread her ashes over her grandpa and grandma's grave. My family, who lived in Arizona at the time, and Charles, went with us. We had a nice service of spreading her ashes and had a prayer meeting after. We then went to dinner at the club on base and had fellowship and remembered Debbie and all that she meant to each one of us.

When we got home that night, we called Brad and Kathie, telling them what we had done and where we had spread their mom's ashes. They were happy that her ashes were finally in a resting place. God is so good! He allowed us to mend the feelings that Charles had carried with him so that we all could be together on this day. I thank God for working it all out.

Lynn Stephens

My mother's heart still aches to hold her, to talk with her, and to love on her. I keep telling the Lord to tell her that we miss her and love her. I thank God that I know without a doubt that she is home in Heaven with Jesus.

CHAPTER FIVE
THE ULTIMATE HEALING

Two weeks after Debbie's memorial service, I felt God's grace slowly lifting off me. This is when I started to question God in earnest. For two weeks I had experienced such an abundance of God's grace, it allowed me to minister to others. His grace was so precious that it is hard to understand. Peace, peace, wonderful peace coming down from the Father above! But this I know—that He is faithful to give you just the right amount of grace for the occasion. I had never experienced it before because I had never needed it before. I believe all believers walk in God's grace and mercy daily to the extent that we need it. But in extreme situations, He pours out His grace to help us through those times. I thank God every day for His precious love and grace.

While under His grace, I fully trusted in what God was doing in Debbie's life, the life of her children, and in our lives. But as the grace lifted, I started to question and talk to God in ways that I hadn't before. I remember one question to God was, "Why, God, didn't you heal her? I have seen you heal many in my presence, why not now?" I believe God knew these questions were in my heart before. He lifted the grace that covered up the questions so I did not see or feel them. But now, He wanted me to see how my faith would hold up. I must be honest with you, I was not mad at God for lifting His grace, or for the questions I wanted answers to. But just the same, I wanted Him to answer. After many mornings and nights of asking Him the same questions over and over again, He finally answered me, and I was taken aback by His answer.

He said, "I took her when I had her." I did not understand.

"God," I said, "What do you mean by that?"

God said, "Lynn, remember your prayers for your children? You have been asking me to save them, no matter what?"

"Yes, I do God."

"Well, now was the time," God told me. "Lynn, if I had healed her on earth, I saw in the future she would have walked away from me. Debbie would have gotten caught back up in the world. But her illness made her see her need for me. So, Lynn, I was honoring your prayers. And Debbie is with me now in all her beauty. She has received her ultimate healing and will never be sick again."

I was amazed. Then I cried out, "But Lord, the children! They need their mom."

I felt His loving arms around me and He said, "Don't you worry about the children, they are in my care. I love them more than you do, Lynn, and I have prepared them for this time." Then, deep in my spirit, I felt a release of Brad and Kathie to God and knew without a doubt that they would be fine. Debbie had lived her life for her children. She had loved them with all her heart and soul and had protected them. Yes, they miss their mother and love her to this day, but they have gone on, and I see God's hand on their lives, protecting them. God has taken over for Debbie. I know that today she is a very proud mother as she looks down upon them from Heaven. So many times we think God is not hearing our prayers, but I am here to tell you that he is very involved in every minute of every day of our lives.

I praised God for His wisdom and asked him to forgive me for the questions. But He did not mind for He wants an intimate relation with all of us. When you are intimate with one another, you sometimes question each other. Oh, I remember quite a few times God has questioned me, saying, "Lynn, what on earth are you doing?" Or, "Lynn, do you really think I wanted you to do that?"

This mother's heart is at peace, and I continue to pray that same prayer for the rest of my family, yet I hope they do not have to go through such a trial as Debbie did to run their race. God is so good, and He knows how to get, not only our attention, but the attention of our family and love ones. Keep on praying and never let go of His hem. God does heal, but not always in the ways we think He should perform that healing. Isaiah 53:5 says, "But he was pierced for our transgressions, He was crushed for our iniquities; the punishment that brought us peace was upon Him, *and by His wounds we ARE healed.*" Not maybe healed, but that we *are* healed. James 5:14 says, "Is any one of you sick? He should call the elders of the church to pray over him and anoint him with oil in the name of the Lord. And the prayer offered in faith will make the sick person well; the Lord will raise him up. If he has sinned, he will be forgiven."

These scriptures are very comforting to me, and I stand upon God's word for my healing.

Everyone that came into the room prayed for Debbie's healing. God heard those prayers and honored them. He gave Debbie the ultimate healing because her race was run and it was her time to receive the prize. She is in glory and more beautiful that she was down here on this earth. How could we ask her to come back? That would be selfish on our part. Yes, we miss her presence in our everyday life, but what would that life had been for her if she had stayed? God knew and did what was best for her. Since her going home, I have been able to minister to others who have lost children like no one else could who had not experienced it for themselves. We must not wait to have our faith strengthened through trials, but we must strive to have a strong faith on a daily basis. Then, when tragedy and sorrow come, we are strong enough to stand on God's promises and strength. From the time Debbie went into the hospital, I confessed my weakness to the Lord to go through whatever was ahead and asked Him to please take over, hold me in His loving arms, and carry me through that time of trouble. He did! He was faithful to my request and He will be to yours, no matter how strong your faith is. But it will be so much easier to trust in Him if your faith is already strong. About two weeks after the memorial service, when I felt the heavy anointing grace lift off me, it was God setting me back

on my feet as He had been holding me the whole time.
I reflect back to the poem *Footprints in the Sand.*

Footprints in the Sand

One night I dreamed I was walking
along the beach with the Lord.
Many scenes from my life flashed across the sky.
In each scene I noticed footprints in the sand.
Sometimes there were two sets of footprints,
other times there was one only.
This bothered me because I noticed that
during the low periods of my life,
when I was suffering from anguish,
sorrow or defeat,
I could see only one set of footprints,
so I said to the Lord,
"You promised me, Lord,
that if I followed you,
you would walk with me always.
But I have noticed that during the
most trying periods of my life
there has only been one set of footprints in the sand.
Why, when I needed you most, have
you not been there for me?"

The Lord replied,
"The years when you have seen
only one set of footprints,
my child, is when I carried you."

This was definitely one scene in our lives when Jesus was holding both Wayne and I. He had given me grace to minister to others, and Wayne had grace, as a man, to show his deepest grief to those around him, which allowed them to be able to express their grief also. Nothing is accidental with God. He has a plan for each one of us, and the plan for my life is not the same as the plan for your life. Faith is trusting completely in God and relying on and obeying His Word.

As adults we are prepared to one day put the senior members of our family to rest. Yes, there was mourning when our parents passed away, but we expected that we would see that day in our life. However, a child is something that just does not compute in our minds--that they would leave this world before us. It is not something that we can easily get our minds to accept, the fact that they are gone. When it happens, it can devastate a person, a couple, a family, and a community if they do not know the Lord and the surety that there is a Heaven and a life after death. We are not vapor that ceases to exist when we pass through the valley of death. God's word tells us that Jesus lives and is in heaven preparing a place for us.

> *John 14:1-4. Jesus says, "Do not let your hearts be troubled. Trust in God, trust also in me. In my Father's house are many rooms; if it were not so, I would have told you. I am going there to prepare a place for you. And if I go and prepare a place for you, I will come back and take you to be with me that you also may be where I am. You know the way to the place where I am going."*

> *Then, in verses six and seven: Jesus says, "I am the way and the truth and the life. No one comes to the Father except through me. If you really knew me, you would know my Father as well. From now on, you do know him and have seen him."*

The purpose for writing this book is to bring comfort to those who have lost children and to encourage them in the Lord. He is the only way we can get through this tragic loss with joy in our hearts. Knowing that God loves and cares for me, and that He allowed this to be in my life for a purpose, gives me hope that the result will be worth whatever pain that we have endured. I look at Debbie's children, Brad and Kathie, and I see their lives as they are today. They now know their father's side of the family as they knew us the first eleven and thirteen years. This was important to Debbie and something she wanted for her children when they were old enough to fend for themselves. When the children asked to stay with their dad that summer before she died, she was sad as she would miss them, but she had confided in me that this was right. Debbie knew they were old enough to handle the relationships. They needed to build that relationship back into their life. I know that after Debbie's death, they may have felt some guilt with the fact that they had not been with her, but they have no reason to. Their mother had always loved their father, for together, they had the children, and their presence is a blessing for us all. It is sad that love can survive a divorce, but it does. They had their mother's blessing to stay, and she would not want them to be discouraged about their quest to stay and renew the relationships with their dad and family.

The Word tells us that this life is a blink of the eye compared to eternal life with God. We are here for just a moment and have one chance to get it right. Our life on earth is preparing for eternity with God, ruling and reigning with Jesus. We are to grow in love with God more everyday and know his Word and obey his precepts. Then we will be prepared to go into the future with God, which is in Heaven. I have seen the despair of people who have no hope. They think that death is the final chapter, but in fact, it is the beginning of what life was always meant to be. In this age of trying to blot God out of the world, the despair among people is growing in epic speed. Their hope is gone. Their joy is nonexistent, and they try to find these things through material things. However, only God can fill the place that He put in our hearts to house His spirit.

Lynn Stephens

My prayer is that this little book about my daughter will bring you comfort. I pray it will bring you closer to God and that you will find the joy and the peace that you long for in His word. May God richly abundantly bless all who read the life's story of our daughter, Deborah Anne! God has truly blessed me for sharing it with you.

CHAPTER SIX
A MEMORIAL TO DEBBIE

As I close out this labor of love, I wanted to share some of what people said at the memorial service and in their cards. To hear what others thought of Deborah Anne is so important for the ending to this story.

My husband, Wayne, was not able to stand and give a testimony, so he wrote one out and one of our brothers in Christ read it.

> *Thank you, church, for loving Debbie! You know fathers have a special type of love relationship with their children. The same as mothers bring a love relationship that is different and nurturing. It takes both with the Lord to make the family circle complete.*
>
> *When a son marries and leaves home, there is a feeling of independence. He's a man, but he's on his own. But when a daughter marries and*

leaves home, it is not the same. She is always your little girl. She is never too grown up to sit on your lap, hug your neck, or call you daddy.

Children are a gift from God, but through them He shows us earthly fathers what treasures are here and for eternity:

Love from the Father above, love of a wife, and Love of your children, and nothing else really matters.

So, Debbie, while I am here, I will miss your presence. I will cherish your memories of the good times and hard times. I will continue to see you in Kathie and Brad. But I'll know we will be together again some day because you're with our Lord and Savior.

I love you Debbie, regardless how I look at the memorial service, I am rejoicing at your homecoming.

When I got up to speak, I read the poem that you saw at the beginning of this book. I then said the following:

Our children and grandchildren are our life. Next to the Lord, their salvation and well being has been Wayne and my only concern.

Debbie was our first gift from God and on October 30, 1996, at 5:10 PM after thirty-three years of life on earth, we gave that gift back to the Father. We wanted to keep her, and her children wanted to keep her, but God wanted her home to be with Him. Although we are grieving for the loss of her physical presence, wonderful love, companionship, her relationship, humor, and her caring ways, we are rejoicing today that she is with Jesus, for in March of this year, she gave her heart to the Lord. The pastor at our church let Wayne baptise her and from that time on, we saw her grow these last months into a woman who loved the Lord and showed His love through her.

137

> *I think her message to those who are here today is this: If you do not know Jesus as your personal Savior and if you are not trusting in Him only for your journey to heaven after death then come forward now and allow the pastor and I to pray for you to receive Jesus.*

Here is what Kathie, Debbie's daughter, read. She was eleven years old at the time.

> *I know my mom is in heaven,*
> *The angels took her there.*
> *With loving arms God welcomed her,*
> *And now she's in His care.*
>
> *I know that Heaven is beautiful,*
> *Where the purest waters flow.*
> *I know that mom is healthy now,*
> *The Bible tells me so.*
>
> *Jesus promised to stay beside me,*
> *Along my path today.*
> *Please let your angels surround me,*
> *And guide me on my way.*

Help me, God, to remember,
That mom is in your care.
Help me, God, to remember,
Someday we'll meet her there.

Karen, Debbie's cousin, read for Debbie from Heaven to Kathie's thoughts.

Death is not a dreary thing,
As sad as it may seem.
Heaven is more wonderful,
That in my fondest dream.

I'd like to tell you all about it,
You'd get excited, too.
Everything is bright and shiny
There's so many things to do.

I feel no grief, I feel no pain,
There's only beauty here.
I'm happier than ever before,
With my Lord so dear.

Yes, I'm gone from earth, and yet,
Don't be sad for me.

This is a wonderful place to be,
And someday you will see.

Make sure your heart is right with God,
So you can come here, too.
We'll be together someday soon,
I'm waiting here for you!

By Wanda L. Brey. Written for Debbie's memorial service.

Sandra Shaffer, a friend in Christ, read the following:

I join you in your sorrow at the passing of Debbie, my friend and my sister in Jesus Christ.

The Bible tells us that "life is as a vapor that appeareth for awhile and vanishes away."
In Debbie's short life, she did a major thing. She responded to the drawing of the Holy Spirit and accepted Jesus Christ as her Lord and Savior, and now she has entered into eternal life with Him.

Deborah Anne, God's Blessing

This Sunday, we as a church will gather together and we will miss Debbie being in our midst, but as we worship and praise Jesus in the spirit, Debbie will worship and praise God in His presence. What she believed in her heart she now sees with her eyes.

When I left her hospital room on Wednesday afternoon, I could not say goodbye. I said, "Debbie, I will see you in the morning," and I did not mean Thursday morning. And I now say to Debbie again, "We love you! Look for us; we will see you in the morning."

Sandra

"Death is a Doorway" by Helen Steiner Rice

On the wings of death
The soul takes flight
Into the land
Where there is not night,
For those who believe

Lynn Stephens

> *What the Savior said*
> *Will rise in glory*
> *Though they be dead...*
> *So death comes to us*
> *Just to open the door*
> *To the kingdom of God*
> *And life evermore.*

Our prayers are with you! Paul and Karen Kleewein and Family

Dear Wayne and Lynn,

We hurt and grieve with you and know what you are going through. Love and prayers, Myrtle and Marion Graves. (This precious couple truly knew what we were going through as they lost their son, who was a policeman, in the line of duty.)

> *This world, however beautiful, was never meant to be*
> *The place that we would call our home for all eternity.*

Deborah Anne, God's Blessing

And though we would not choose to leave, a loving God knows best,

And in His time He lifts us to a place of peace and rest.

For He has built a mansion where His children will abide

Free from pain and sorrow, forever at His side.

He said He'd never leave us to face our trials alone,

And though sometimes we fail Him, He never fails His own.

And even when our choices are less than He would ask,

He knows when human courage is unequal to the task.

We cannot judge what happens, though tears and questions start,

We only see what's visible—God sees into the heart.

And though there may be many things that we cannot explain,

We can be sure it breaks His heart to see His children's pain.

In loving arms He bears us to a quiet place apart

Where He mends the wounded spirit and heals the broken heart.

And though these ones we love so much have left our present sight

And passed into a better world of majesty and light,

Someday we'll be together in our Father's home above

Where we'll thank Him for His mercy and praise Him for his Love.

A poem by Kay Andrew from a sister in Christ, Charlotte Cates:

Deborah Anne, God's Blessing

God knows there will be sorrow,
So He gives us tears to cry,
He knows there will be trials
When His children ask Him, "Why?"

But He's our Heavenly Father,
And He'll take us by the hand
To lead us through the sorrows
That we cannot understand.

God has all the time we need—
He feels the pain we feel,
And He, above all others,
Knows a heart takes time to heal

With Deepest Sympathy in the Loss of Your Daughter

Just like a beautiful long-stemmed rose,
Her precious memory grows and grows,
Touching the hearts of all of those she loved.

145

And like the fragrance of that same rose,

Her love, so sweet, still flows and flows,

Filling our lives with a warmth

That shows she's there.

So like a forever-blooming rose,

The beauty she shared eternally glows,

For deep in our hearts

Each of us knows she lives!

"She was a great mother, sister, and daughter, and we will always love her. I just really miss her and everyone knows that." Bradley Thomas Hamilton, Deborah's son

---

From our dear friend in Christ, who has since passed away, and is with Debbie now. Lucille Blanton.

The Rose Beyond the Wall

A rose once grew where all could see,
Sheltered beside a garden wall.
And, as the days passed swiftly by,
It spread its branches, straight and tall...

Deborah Anne, God's Blessing

One day, a beam of light shone through
A crevice that had opened wide
The rose bent gently toward its warmth
Then passed beyond to the other side ...

Now, you who deeply feel its loss,
Be comforted—the rose blooms there—
Its beauty even greater now,
Nurtured by God's own loving care.

A message signed by many attendees to the memorial service:

We feel so sad when those we love
Are called to live with God above,
But why should we grieve
When they say goodbye
And go to dwell in a cloudless sky?
For they have but gone to prepare the way,
And we'll meet them again some happy day,
For God has told us that nothing can sever
A life He created to live on forever ...
So let God's promise soften our sorrow
And give us new strength
For a brighter tomorrow.
By Helen Steiner Rice

Jesus, *The Shepherd*, sent to us from a dear friend and coworker in a ministry that shows to the world His love. From Katherine Genders, Founder and Director of the *Simon Peter Passion Play of Tucson.*

> *Not one shall be lost*
> *Of the lambs in His fold,*
> *For Jesus the Shepherd*
> *Calls each one His own...*
> *Not one shall be lost*
> *Though they pass through the gate,*
> *Departing from earth*
> *And the life they have known...*
> *Not one shall be lost*
> *Though we see them no more,*
> *For a wonderful Shepherd*
> *Is calling them there,*
> *And He'll lead them by name*
> *Into heavenly fields,*
> *And keep them forever*
> *In His loving care.*

Those are just a few of the many cards and sentiments that we received from our friends. They were extremely encouraging to us in our time of sorrow, and if you are going through a loss of a child, young or old, my prayer is that they will give you some comfort. As you lean on the Lord, His strength will encircle you. There has to be a bigger reason for this incredible tragedy, and though it's hard to fully make sense out of it, we have to believe that God is at work in our lives, and when we see Him face to face, then and only then will we know His purpose.

Love Always and Forever in Jesus,
Lynn Stephens

Printed in the United States
40459LVS00001B/136-159